HAPPY ENDINGS

RAW AND HONEST STORIES FROM A MOM
SEARCHING FOR EXCITEMENT
AND FINDING FULFILLMENT

JANA SMITH

HAPPY ENDINGS:
Raw and Honest Stories from a Mom Searching for Excitement and Finding Fulfillment

Published by Solus Press, Cincinnati, Ohio
Printed in the United States of America

ISBN 979-8-9894979-1-1 (print)

Table of Contents

Introduction

Every woman has a story.

While working full time as a hospitality executive, I was asked why I had decided to write a book, more specifically, why did I write this book? My answer was exactly that: every woman has a story. Whether that story ends with a happy ending or not, it is your own unique story. It has shaped the woman that you are today. There is absolutely no reason that we shouldn't be able to live out our own story, on our own terms, with no regrets and no explanations.

Whether that story takes you your whole life to realize, or you start to notice it early on, we all have one that we should embrace. Then we must decide what to do with that story. We can stay quiet, allowing it to shape us in a definitive but silent way, or we can embrace all of the many chapters and share it with the world. Either way is not wrong, it is just different. At the ripe age of forty-eight, I have decided to share my story with all of you. I hope that by being real, being bold, and being as truthful as I can be, it will inspire someone else to tell theirs.

My love of writing has always been there. Even as a kid, I loved to write short action-adventure stories. I guess in some ways now I am still writing about action and adventure, just this time it is my real life. It is amazing to me how easily my thoughts and memories flowed onto the paper, almost in a therapeutic manner. I would catch myself smiling as I recalled certain memories, allowing myself to pause from writing and savor the entire memory. Being divorced and getting back into the dating world seems easy enough to most, but when you are living it, it can be a lonely and scary time in your life. While one chapter is ending, some are just getting started. Being able to now share that significant part of my life is freeing and empowering. For so long I had been hiding those years, when I should had been sharing them.

A lot of women have secrets, whether it's a sexual fantasy that will ever live only in your mind, or a real-life, lust-filled romance that you are searching to find. This is why romance novels are bestsellers—we can relate to the escape. It wasn't until after my divorce that I decided to explore my own sexual fantasies that sadly most would deem as inappropriate for women. Stuck in a hypercritical society where men are applauded for multiple partners and women are shunned, I decided to create my own path and satisfy my own desires. I started chasing my passion and left behind the insecurity of the what-ifs.

Where did I get the courage to put these memories into a book and share them with the world? I don't think I could pinpoint the exact moment. I just knew that during the process of just being whoever I wanted to be, I started caring less about what others think. I started focusing on myself and my adventure and living my own life instead of what everyone else would have wanted me to be.

Every woman has a story. Thank you for reading mine. May you laugh and feel inspired to live your own.

Chapter 1

I am a very responsible person and a good mother, so there is no way that wild and crazy sex thoughts should be racing through my head. Only those women who are carefree, slutty, and wild did naughty, kinky things. Every day, I put on my sensible pumps and business suit while listening to the Wiggles in the car on the way to daycare. Getting hot and bothered with thoughts of swingers' parties and bondage was not part of the scheduled plan. But guess what—those thoughts were there, and I could either ignore them the rest of my life or do something about it. Somehow, waiting until everyone left the house, pulling out my smutty romance novel and my trusty vibrator just wasn't enough anymore. I was about to embark on a secret journey that would uncover these taboo topics and introduce me to a life that I had never known. A life that would satisfy my wildest cravings.

Romance novels account for 18 percent of adult fiction sales, making it the second most popular fiction genre overall. Eighty-two percent of these readers are women. Forty-five percent of romance readers have a college degree and on average are forty-two years old. So, you can roll your eyes at the thought of reading one, or even secretly hide one under your pillow for when you are alone, but it is a fact that there is a significant demand for these cheesy romantic novels. You all know the types of books I am speaking of...rich, beautiful, sexy people filled with unbridled passion and sweaty lust. Passionate lovemaking with no awkward moments, no wondering if you look fat in this position. These books make us think that a women can have multiple orgasms with just a touch of a man's hand. Not even close.

With that many romance books being sold, I firmly believe that many average women secretly yearn for the opportunity to live our lives like this, or to at least experience it once or twice in our lifetime. To experience hot, writhing, dirty sex with no complications. To get kinky and not worry about your partner looking at you like you're crazy for suggesting such a thing. Deep inside, we all have a fetish or fantasy, but most likely it will never be acted upon. Have you ever wondered what a threesome is like? Or to feel the beautiful curves of another woman? Selfishly, I know these thoughts had crossed my mind a time or two, but as quickly as they would come up, I would bury them back down where they belonged. A classy, self-respecting woman should never have thoughts like these, and should only conduct herself with the utmost grace and dignity. Guess what, I believe you can do both! Here I am, a middle-aged, recently divorced woman, mom of a four-year-old daughter with a successful career in hospitality. I do not look like the supermodels on the pages of fashion magazines, nor do I look like the girls on *Girls Gone Wild.*

Getting divorced at thirty-five, I felt like a giant failure. I truly thought I would be married forever, just as everyone does in the beginning. I always told myself that divorce wasn't even an option. It turns out it is an option, and one that I opted for. My ex-husband is a wonderful father to our daughter, but he was not the right life partner for me. Admitting that to myself was probably one of the hardest things I had ever done. I take that back; actually telling him that I was no longer in love with him and leaving was even harder. I questioned myself about a hundred times, trying to think of creative ways to make it work, what damage was this going to do to my daughter. Should I stay married for her? You name it, I thought of it. We were married for a total of five years. In the beginning, life was great, as it usually is. That's how you think it's always going to be. We traveled the world together and ate great food in the countries we visited. Our sex life was on par for a married couple (or what I thought was on par). We made love maybe once a week, and though it was not eventful, it was decent and served its purpose. He is twenty-three years older than me, and at first, love was truly blind. The age difference felt nonexistent. We welcomed our daughter almost exactly a year after we were married and became your normal family of three. Both of us were making decent money, dinner was eaten together at the table in the evenings, we had a beautiful home, and two SUVs. Life as I knew it was good.

A couple of years into the marriage, things shifted. The energy that we had both had early in our marriage had quickly faded, giving way to evenings on the couch in front of the TV. Our life became stagnant and boring. I longed for the days of travel, road trips, outings, and fun. Instead, it was filled with what TV show we should watch that night and what should we eat for dinner or snacks. Weight gain hit both of us hard, which caused me to be depressed and resentful. Bedtime was at nine p.m. sharp, but not to have sex, to actually go to sleep. The age difference between us became a huge issue, as now he was a fifty-six-year-old man, and I was thirty-four, just when a woman starts coming into her own, reaching her sexual peak. Speaking of sex, it had become so infrequent, and when it did happen it typically lasted the length of a commercial break with nonexistent passion. Missionary style with no lust, no talking—hurry up and finish. Even then, sometimes it even ended without finishing. Disappointing and lonely in a marriage. That is how I felt.

Knowing deep inside that I needed more, I decided that first I needed to take care of myself. I started working out, losing forty pounds, and started feeling like my old self as well as a new woman. With my confidence starting to reach new heights, I pleaded with my husband that we had to find the passion that we once had, passion that I knew existed, and that I longed for. I wanted my marriage to work for many reasons, most of all because we had vowed to stay together. I was honest with him, telling him I needed to feel lust, I needed to feel desired. I lost track of how many times I literally begged for him to spontaneously throw me on the kitchen counter and rock my world. To surprise me with any type of romance would have helped the situation, or even just to spend five minutes of foreplay before we made love. When I would tell him these things, he would laugh and tell me I was being silly, then quickly brush off the comment as if it was never mentioned. Soon, I gave up asking. What was the point? I felt trapped. Would I stay in a sexless marriage and continue to coexist with my husband as a roommate for the rest of my life?

After few months, I finally came to the realization that my marriage was over. There was no saving it, and honestly, I no longer wanted to save it. I was miserable. We hadn't had sex in almost a year. I was wearing out my vibrator's batteries almost every week. I didn't even recognize the man he had become: a stranger in the house. We hardly spoke anymore, and if we did, it was only to discuss the daily happenings of our daughter. Deep down I truly knew that I didn't love him anymore. There was no attraction. I longed to be happy and feel satisfied in all aspects of my life. I knew if I stayed, not only would I let myself down, but I feel that ultimately I would have let my daughter down. It was important for me to show my daughter the understanding of life is short and you need to be fulfilled with happiness.

Moving out of our home was brutal for everyone. I loved our home so very much. It was the home that we brought our newborn daughter to and where sweet memories of her growing up had been made. It was also the house that our marriage ended in. Trying to convince myself that things would get better and

I was doing the right thing, I knew that I would someday have another house hopefully filled with even more love and laughter. Sweating and tired, I filled my moving boxes, stacked them in the U-Haul, and drove away.

Slightly terrified, but also slightly empowered, I offered my daughter, the love of my life, a weak smile in the rearview mirror as we drove down the street to start our new chapter. It was time to live my life on my terms.

Chapter 2

Year one of being divorced sucks. To me, it was like experiencing a death. The person that you were with every day is now never by your side. Your bed is empty. Your heart is empty and a bit jaded about love. I felt sad and slightly like a loser for quitting on my marriage, questioning myself repeatedly if I really did the right thing. Then once the sadness faded, the anger started to set in. It was difficult to realize how hard I had tried to make my marriage work, but, in the end, it takes two people, not just the one. I also realized how much of my life I had given to this person, now wasted. My daughter, the highlight of my life, was the best and only thing to come out of my marriage.

Once I passed through the sadness and anger stages, I realized it was finally time to move on. Online dating was fairly new at this time, and definitely wasn't as accepted and mainstream as it is today. I was even embarrassed to admit to my family and friends that I was going to give it a try. As a woman with a busy career and a tireless four-year-old at home, I was not about to spend my evenings at a bar hoping to find a date, so this was my best option. Plus, I figured online dating was a lot like shopping, which always has been one of my favorite pastimes. How hard could it be?

Sitting down one evening, I was going to attempt to create a profile on Match.com. Logging in, I thought I'd peruse a few ads to get inspiration for my own profile. Everything I read was about finding your true love and looking for a relationship. It hadn't even been a year since I had been divorced, and honestly, a committed relationship was the last thing I wanted or needed. My brain and my body were sexually frustrated. I needed to get laid. It had been almost two years since I had sex. Two years! For a woman coming into her sexual peak, that was far too long. Hell, who am I kidding, that was too long for a woman who wasn't even in her sexual peak!

I had to seriously ask myself: What did I really want? What did I need both physically and mentally? My whole life I had been taught that sex comes with feelings, and that to have sex you must be in a committed relationship. To have multiple partners as a woman made you a slut; multiple partners as a man made you a stud. What a tragic double standard. What would happen if I lived my life like those romance novels? A life filled with passion, excitement, lust. It would be my secret, something I would tell no one. Like living a double life, which made my stomach start to tingle with excitement. It was time to have some fun. Naughty fun.

Quickly I realized that Match.com was not going to be able to meet my needs. It was out. It didn't align with what I was looking for at this stage in my life. Maybe one day it would benefit me, but not now. I needed to find a site that fostered and promoted my sexual desires. A site where I wouldn't be judged for my thoughts and could explore a side of myself that I had never tapped into but had always wanted to. I found a site called Adult Friend Finder, or AFF. I quickly realized I had not mentally prepared myself for what I was about to see. Anything goes within the walls of this website. Basically, this was a hookup site for sex. Pictures galore! Immediately my senses were highly stimulated…arousal, fear, excitement. This was uncharted territory, and I was already loving it.

Step one was easy; log in and password were created. Step two was much harder; describing myself and what I was looking for, or rather into. As I had done before, I decided to browse several other profiles, looking for inspiration before feeling ready to start my own. People of all shapes, sizes, and colors were looking for satisfaction, with absolutely no fear of letting everyone know what turned them on. Literally, a door was opened into the world of sexual fantasy turning into real life. Before I knew it, I had clocked several hours of just reading and browsing. Each profile was so intriguing, and they all seemed so confident. I really couldn't wait to be a part of this. Slowly, I began to write my profile, "Average woman looking for a good time, no strings attached." I deleted it. Too boring. I needed to jump in with both feet, not just dip my foot in the pool. I needed to sound like I know what I'm doing and I was as confident as these other people. If I was going to do this, I needed to go for it.

"Recently divorced, sexual frustrated woman looking for an amazing time. It's been two years, so I am ready to get my world rocked. Searching for a one-time hookup with no strings attached, and maybe twice if you earn it. Willing to try most things. No virgins…I need experience. Bring it! Cum satisfy me." Chuckling, and nodding my head in approval, I hit submit.

Now for the profile picture. For a second, I hesitated, wondering what if I put a picture on this site and someone recognizes me. I quickly dismissed my worry, remembering the people that I had just looked at on the website. They were different people than the ones I hung out with and worked with daily. What were the chances that classy, upstanding people were on this site? Right? Also thinking, I may not get any hits if I didn't include a picture, so I decided it was best to put one on. But frighteningly enough, what if I got no hits with my picture? That would be humiliating. I really did think I stood a chance to get some responses, even if not a lot of them, especially noting that there were both men and women of all kinds on the site. Mostly trashy and naked; however, some so gorgeous that you would swear it had to be a fake picture. I think of myself somewhere in-between. Don't get me wrong, I think I am very average-looking, even decent-looking, but I wouldn't go as far as saying I had sex appeal. I am five four, 150 pounds, blond hair, and blue eyes. Professional-looking is maybe the best way to describe me—not trashy, but again, not sexy.

Googling how to take a sexy picture of oneself, I found all the examples extremely humorous. Push the booty out, pout the lip, show some cleavage. Good lord, this was more challenging than writing the profile paragraph. Also, trying to find something sexy to wear in this photo would be a feat. Nothing I owned was revealing or low cut. I think if I searched, I might be able to find the only piece of sexy lingerie I ever owned, but that was probably ten years old at best. Searching through my current photos (on my flip phone), I looked for one that could possibly work.

Maybe if it was innocent enough, I could possibly get more responses. Leaving more to the imagination was sexy, wasn't it? Finally, I found one that I didn't hate. It was a recent picture of me in shorts and a tank top posing with my cousin's dog on my lap. There was no sexiness about it, but at least you could see my figure and smile. And my hair was on point. That was important. Time to jump in. I uploaded the photo and clicked submit. Then I waited.

Chapter 3

One hundred and twenty-seven emails!

Are you freaking kidding me? Waking up the next morning, I immediately signed in to the site and was shocked to see the flood of responses. Now, before I sound cocky, let me set the stage that on these sites, the ratio of single women to single men is extremely low. But that being said, wow! I grabbed a cup of coffee, still in my pajamas, I started perusing.

By jumping in with both feet, I quickly learned the rules and guidelines of being on an adult website. You can "flirt" with someone by clicking on a small heart on their profile. This sends them an update that you are interested in what you see, but you want to know if the feeling is mutual. It encourages them to make the next move. You can also send them an email that appears only in your platform inbox located on the site. Nothing goes to your personal email, as that is highly protected unless you give it directly to someone. Lastly, while you are active on the site, you can online chat with another member. Browsing through my incoming emails, I noticed a constant pinging sound of online members trying to catch my attention and chat. It was all a bit overwhelming in the beginning to navigate through. I found myself not being able to keep up with a conversation before another one would begin.

People from all walks of life had responded to my profile. Mostly single men, but women and couples were also interested in me and had sent emails. I learned that for twenty emails someone sends out, they may get two to three responses back. It was a bit like fishing. And if you didn't like the conversation, you just threw it back, like a fish you didn't want. I also learned that most of the men on the site were oddly similar. Most profile pictures were dick pics. I don't know about you, but penises are not the prettiest thing to look at. A big dick might be very alluring, but only after you have seen its owner's face to know if he is attractive or not. As a girl, I must have physical attraction before I can even consider having sex with someone. Good looks were definitely on my must-have list of criteria.

Speaking of my criteria… Seeing the responses I had received, and conversations that were developing, I quickly had to decide what would make the list of acceptable versus deal-breakers. The previous night, I had prepared myself not to be picky, but seeing the volume of responses, I now knew I could afford to be choosy. Good looks, as I had mentioned earlier, were a must. Then there had to be an attraction and chemistry. If I didn't feel anything, no sparks, what was the point? Chemistry started early. I had to feel something different, a spark of some sort, within the first few minutes of the conversation. Not only did they need to turn me on, but I hoped that they were able to make me laugh and hold a conversation. But ultimately, I wanted to feel the desire to rip their clothes off—again, the main reason of starting down this path. I was determined to find the passion and lust that I so desired.

Another item on the list: safety. I took many precautions for my journey to stay safe, not only for birth control, but not to get murdered or chopped up into bits. (I've read many stories.) Obviously, no one was ever allowed to my home, nor would I meet them directly at their place. Keep in mind, video chatting wasn't a thing yet, so to know if it was really the even the person you thought it was, you found out in your first meeting. Lastly, always meeting in a public place was key and felt much safer. The last bit of the criteria on my list was looking at the fetishes that they were into. Did it align with things that turned me on or things that I wanted to try? There were also fetishes that were a hard no for me, so that eliminated those people right off the bat. Intense pain, golden showers, sex with animals were no-nos.

One of the major differences in an adult sex site versus a regular dating site (besides the obvious) was the fact that you really don't have to make small talk. Surprisingly enough, I found this oddly satisfying. You could easily jump into a sexual conversation with someone to find out quickly if you were sexually compatible. This weeded out so many people right off the bat. Now don't get me wrong, carrying on a conversation was still very important, but the topics that were always taboo to speak about when first meeting someone were now coming up first. Most of the conversations always started with "What are you looking for on this website?" and "What are you into?" This aided in weeding out those that did not make a match. I did the love the fact that no matter what you listed as what you were into, no one judged you. Well, at least not in the conversation or to your face.

Starting out timidly and a little shy in these conversations, I quickly gained the confidence I needed to succeed in this arena. Talking graphically about what you want done to you by someone you have never met is quite daunting as well as thrilling.

Continuing to weed through emails, I deleted the ones that didn't immediately spark a feeling of chemistry within me. Cheesy pickup lines were a dime a dozen, and I quickly grew bored with the same ol' stuff. So many men insisted they could make me orgasm like I never had before. Or that they were the best lover ever. Not to be picky, but shouldn't I be the judge of whether you are the best? Plus, you are already creating huge shoes to fill, and what if it is a letdown? Then that looks even worse on you. Men also don't understand that it can be tough for women to orgasm. Orgasming is not like what you read about in romance novels. It takes concentration, a level of comfort—not to mention someone who really knows what they are doing in that area to happen. But when it does, look out.

From the remaining candidates, it was eye-opening and erotic to chat with these strangers. I found myself getting caught up in late-night erotic conversations that would literally have me touching myself while on the phone. Further intrigued by a handful of the men, I shared my phone number for easier communication and texting. Sexting was my new thing that began happening at all hours of the day. I felt like a schoolgirl again. Having this sneaky sexy secret that only I knew drove me wild. It made every encounter and text feel riskier and more dangerous. I loved it.

> *I am proud to say my work and parenting never wavered during these times. I was the same steady, responsible person I always had been, just now with a secret and a sexual desire that I was finally going to allow to be satisfied and quenched.*

By keeping this secret, I was already starting to change on the inside and outside, feeling myself becoming more sexual and confident in my own skin. I was now owning my decision to be the sexual person that I wanted to be.

Out of the ten or so guys that I was sexting with on a regular basis, one stood out to me more than the others. The texting had started out friendly and funny, both traits I am attracted to and hoped I would find in addition to the sexual arousal. He was a fireman who lived across town and was ten years my junior. A fireman! Like in the calendars! His profile picture showed a stout man with a mane of wavy brown hair and washboard abs, posing in just his fireman pants and hat. So hot! Granted, the picture of him alone was a turn-on, but as we continued to get to know each other, the sexual tension was off the charts. He was eager for us to meet, and although I was eager too, this being my first meeting, I was still hesitant. Reminding myself again that I needed to jump in with both feet, I finally gave in. The anticipation was too much to say no to.

Chapter 4

Fireman and I chatted for about a week before he had talked me into meeting him. More of his pictures showed that chiseled body with washboard abs and wavy brown hair. I figured if I had the pick of the litter, I might as well live out some fantasies with the hottest guys. He and I flirted via text, describing what and how we wanted to have sex with each other. I even bought matching set of a black lacy bra and panties. I wanted to be sexy, even if I was more nervous than I was letting on.

That evening, I drove almost forty-five minutes to the Mexican restaurant where I was meeting him. I walked in and saw his beautiful face immediately at the bar. He looked up from his cocktail and greeted me with perfect teeth and that same chiseled body I had seen in the pictures. When I walked over to him, he stood up (he was so tall) and engulfed me into a warm embrace. He smelled of an amazing musky, salty smell, and I immediately wanted every inch of him. He whispered in my ear that he was glad I showed up and he thought I was even better looking in person. My confidence soared.

We sat down at the bar and started chatting like we knew each other. I did notice he purchased my drink, answering my silent question if people on this site do those types of gestures. He was sweet and funny, and oh, so sexy. The fact that we had talked about what we were going to do to each other beforehand now was on auto-repeat in my head. All I could think about was ripping his clothes off. After about an hour and two or three drinks, he asked if I wanted to get out of there. I couldn't get out of my barstool fast enough. He grabbed my hand, and we walked to my car in the parking lot. He climbed into the passenger seat, and before I knew it his tongue was already in my mouth. I was overwhelmed with desire and could feel my body writhing to be touched by him. As we continued to hungrily kiss, both our hands started wandering over the other's body. He whispered to me to move my car to a more deserted area. Nodding in agreement, I quickly drove about two minutes to a nearby deserted park, and it was on. As he continued to kiss me, he simultaneously pulled me into the back seat. There I straddled him, continuing to kiss, grinding on each other like high school kids. Wiggling out of my top and bra, with his help, I pushed my tits into his awaiting mouth. It was the best feeling, and all I could think about was how much I wanted him. Sliding out my jeans, I made a mental note about next time: a skirt and no panties would make this so much easier. He was out of his jeans before I knew it, and I climbed back on top of him, easing my body down onto his stiff, big cock. I cried out, it felt so good. Two years of tightness clenched around him. We moved together, up and down, sweating and steaming up all the windows. His tongue darting in and out of my waiting mouth as we moved. Wanting to change positions, he gently moved me off of him and instructed me to lie down on the seat. He climbed on top of me and pushed into me with amazing force. I grabbed his ass with my hands and pulled him deeper into me. I was loud. I was moaning; it felt so good, and I couldn't help myself. Before I knew it, he pulled out and came on my stomach, breathing as though he had just run a marathon. Sitting up, I wondered if at this point would it be awkward, but quickly I realized it wasn't. We laughed about the frenzy of the sex act while getting dressed and driving back to the parking lot. As he got out of my car, he looked back at me, cupped my face in his hands, gave me a quick kiss, and headed to his car.

As I watched him drive away, I sat there in my car, still wet from our adventure, and still with a smile plastered on my face. Did that really just happen? He felt so amazing. For a fleeting second, I wondered if he had felt the same way. Did I feel wonderful to him? Would he call me again? Shaking my head and laughing at myself, I realized I had to get better at this. I had to stop "being a girl." Enjoy the sex and go home.

The next day, Fireman texted. I can't lie, it felt really good to hear from him. He said he had a great time the night before and he wanted to see me again. My confidence soared. As we recapped the previous evening, we both agreed that had both been so excited that we hadn't lasted too long. For the next time (yes, the next time!), we wanted to explore each other more and take our time. Agreeing to meet up the next weekend on Friday night, he texted me an address, telling me it was his firehouse, asking if I could meet him there. During the week before our second hookup, we kept a steady stream of sexting going… keeping the sexual tension very high.

Friday, I arrived at the fire station. I had thousands of wild butterflies going crazy inside my stomach, such a crazy feeling, and all still so new to me. He came out to my car to greet me, looking dazzling dressed in his fire pants and suspenders with a tight T-shirt. I couldn't take my eyes off of him. He told me to come in, so I followed closely behind, admiring the view as I went along. Leading me to the bright-red fire engine in front of us, he took my hand, and we stepped inside. I thought, No way, this cannot be happening…this is like a fantasy. As he began kissing my neck, he whispered in my ear, "Have you ever been fucked in a fire engine before?" I couldn't speak even if I had wanted to. Smiling, he began to undress me. Honestly, I never thought about anything else while we were in that engine. I didn't think about what if there had been a fire and they needed the truck. Or if others were watching, or around. All I could think about was the lust that had taken over my body. When he stepped out of his pants, I fell to my knees and took his rock-hard cock into my mouth. I could hear him moaning as I softly sucked and licked. It didn't take long before I could taste him as well.

He then laid me down, taking his time with me, licking every inch of my body. I was trembling with pleasure as he slid his cock inside me, fucking me with an intensity that I craved.

We went at it for at least an hour, trying out many different positions and locations within the truck that were physically possible. To this day, it was one of the hottest encounters I have ever experienced. When we were finished, he asked if I had enjoyed myself. All I could do was smile.

Over the next week, Fireman and I texted every other day, always with enough sexy talk to satisfy my evening. Later that week, I texted him just before I went to bed, telling him I wanted to say good night. Once I sent it, I froze in my tracks. I was eerily aware of that familiar feeling. The "girl" feelings were creeping back up, and I knew I didn't want to start down that road. Not now, not with Fireman, not when I was just starting to sow my wild oats and live my life on my own terms. Don't be a chick, I told myself. Act like a dude. I think Fireman might have felt the same way, as we never spoke again. I think we both had gotten what we needed out of our meetings and had satisfied something in both of us.

Chapter 5

Get back on the horse, I told myself. Who's next? Back to the website I went. I found myself chatting until the wee hours of the morning, having so much fun and getting caught up in my newfound sexuality and outgoing personality. My shyness was starting to fade, as a new taboo topic would arise during chatting, and I found myself curious and highly turned on by things I would have never guessed would turn me on. Talking about threesomes, dom and sub fetishes, gang bangs. I wasn't ready to try these new things just yet, but talking about them with strangers, and knowing it was now a possibility, was highly erotic.

I found myself one evening chatting with a guy who was down to earth and extremely sexy in the way he spoke. He was a train conductor, and his runs had him traveling from Portland, Oregon; to Seattle, Washington; several times a month. I instantly was in love with the idea of someone who lived out of town but who came through frequently, like a hot booty call, or a mysterious, sexy stranger in the night. We agreed to meet up on his next trip to Seattle and met at a local dive bar. I walked in, saw him at a nearby table, and pulled up a chair. An awaiting cocktail and his smile were all I needed, as we settled into getting to know each other.

Train Guy was super friendly—and a little shy, which surprisingly enough gave me more courage to be the aggressor. I gulped the last of my cocktail, and as he was speaking, I leaned in and began kissing him. Surprising myself with this action, I was clearly in the mood to throw caution to the wind that night. Happily, he responded eagerly, pulling my body closer to him as we continued to kiss. Once we broke apart, his look of surprise and desire couldn't be missed. Quickly standing up, he threw a twenty-dollar bill on the table, grabbed my hand, and motioned with his free hand that his hotel was just across the street.

My shirt was already completely unbuttoned as we rode the elevator up to his room. His hands were all over my body, and my tongue was racing up and down his neck. As the elevator doors opened, pulling my hand again, he was already taking out his room key. Flinging the door open, we left a trail of clothes to the bed, naked before even reaching it. The lust and the desire to take him were the feelings I had imagined so many times in my head, and now I was elated as it was actually playing out in real life. Train Guy turned me around and bent me over the cheap hotel bed. From behind me, he reached around and grabbed my tits in his hands. With a firm grasp on them, he plunged his cock into me. My body responded with a wetness and an excitement that was almost uncontrollable. As he continued to find his groove, I begged him to go harder and deeper into me. I couldn't get enough of the feeling. As he started to slow, I stood up and pushed him to the bed. Straddling him, I sat down, feeding him into me with my hand. Once he was deep inside, I began to grind against his cock, until he was moaning with pleasure. I continued to grind, putting my knees up, rocking back and forth on him, while my nipples were gently squeezed between his fingers. I felt myself starting to cum and lost myself in the moment of bliss.

We collapsed onto the bed, both sweaty and panting. I leaned over and kissed him good night, got dressed, and left. No cuddling, no commitment, just an encounter that left us both with smiles on our faces and a satisfying soreness in my crotch. Train Guy and I continued to see each other throughout the next year. He would let me know when he was coming to town, and if my schedule allowed, I would happily meet him, naked in the hotel room.

CHAPTER 6

I had taken the plunge and started this exploration, and so far was loving it. Part of me wanted to see how far I could push myself or dig into some unchartered waters (i.e., fetishes). One night as I was online feeling a little daring, I decided to find someone experienced in the dominant submissive fetish world, and see if it might be something that I wanted to dabble in. Regarding this topic, I really had no knowledge of what it was all about. Like a lot of women, I had read *Fifty Shades of Grey* and knew that it turned me on, so I thought there was a possibility of really loving this world. Now, just speaking for myself, being a successful businesswoman and a boss, I grew tired of always having to call the shots. Especially once I had left work for the day, I wanted someone else to make the decisions, to relinquish my power, and have a man dominate me both in and out of the bedroom. To throw me down, tie me up, and have their absolute naughty way with me. It all sounded so sexy and erotic.

Finding someone considered a "dom" was pretty easy online. S&M, bondage, and sub/dom fetishes were quite trendy and popular. Striking up a conversation with one man in particular, he told me that he was an experienced dom, having a plethora of sexual situations that introduced newbies to this world and to their new submissive role. He was attractive and clean-cut, spoke intelligently, and seemed respectable enough that I thought I would throw caution to the wind and take a chance. Telling him I was ready to try this experience, he expressed his excitement and promised I wouldn't be disappointed.

His first order of business within this world was to give me a command. At that moment, his demeanor slightly changed, becoming more intense and less friendly. I responded eagerly, enjoying the switch and playing into the part. He told me I must answer all of his orders with a "Yes, Master," and then I was to complete the command I was given. The first command, he wanted me to wear a sexy pair of red panties to work the next day and send him a picture of myself in them while at my desk. My heart was pounding as I really had never been told what to do, especially sexually. Still enjoying the moment and the task at hand, I replied, "Yes, Master."

Getting dressed the next morning, I was fully aware of the red lacy panties I had slipped on underneath my skirt. I already felt myself getting wet with excitement, thinking of him and how he would respond to my picture and what my next command might be. After a morning meeting, I retreated to my office, where I shut the door and contemplated the best angle for the picture. As I am always worried about my safety, I definitely was not going to show my face, only a panty shot as he had requested. I think I snapped over twenty pictures, all in different positions, trying to find the sexiest and flattering one to send.

Again, taking pictures of myself never seemed like a sexy task, but I was determined to make this as sensual as possible. Hitting *send* on the best of the worst pictures, I anxiously awaited his response.

Trying to focus on work was tough; this was one of the few times work didn't distract me from personal items. This was my first time exploring this type of relationship, as well as the first time I had sent a "sexy" picture to someone, and from my office no less! I kept checking my phone for a text response, but no such luck. As I was packing up items to go home for the day, I heard the familiar ping of an incoming text message. Quickly grabbing my phone, I saw his number on my screen. "Good girl," was his response. That was it. No comment, and no compliment or critique. The suspense of his thoughts was making me anxious.

With my daughter at her dad's that evening, I helped myself to my usual glass of wine and curled up in my favorite chair with my laptop and phone. I texted him, asking what he had thought about the picture and what I could expect next. I received a quick response, but not what I had hoped to hear. He told me, "Did I tell you to text me? You can wait until I am ready to speak with you." I was a little stunned at his response, and not to mention little hurt. What an ass, I thought. Then, thinking more about what was transpiring, I realized that this was part of the experience. He was controlling the situation, controlling the anticipation and the suspense. The more intense the suspense was, the more sexual it was supposed to become. While I loved the idea of someone else in charge, the suspense thing I could really live without. But again, being all into this exploration, I was up for the challenge.

I didn't hear from him all evening. I went to bed, hoping that I might hear back by tomorrow, as I had no idea how long he would play this out. Waking up in the morning, I checked my phone, and sure enough I had a text from him. This one read, "For today's assignment, I want you to masturbate in your car for me. Masturbate until completion. Get this on video and send it to me. That is all." I reread the message several times to ensure that I had understood him correctly. As I continued to ponder his request, I got up and ready for work. My phone alerted me to a new message, and it was him again. "What do you say?" Day two, and I was already a little over this game. "Yes, Master," I responded, with much less enthusiasm than I had the previous day.

Driving to work, my thoughts again were consumed by his request. Parking in my usual spot in the parking garage, I put my car in park and thought about masturbating. I wasn't feeling the need to touch myself at the moment. I cannot speak for all women, but the act of masturbating with my hand didn't do much for me. I should have brought my vibrator if I wanted any possible shot of completing the task, but I hadn't thought about it. Shaking my head and dismissing the task, I grabbed my purse and headed into the office. Maybe I would try this again on my commute home.

I really didn't think about Master at this point, and went about my busy day. It wasn't until I climbed into my car that his command sprang back into my mind. I drove home, trying to think dirty, erotic thoughts, enough to excite me enough to want to touch myself. Even when I pulled into my driveway, I still didn't have the desire I needed to masturbate. I texted him at this point and said, "I think I failed at the task. We should cut the games and just meet up." Texting back about an hour later, I think he sensed my lack of enthusiasm for this task. He agreed to meet up with me and told me he would send me a note tomorrow about when and where. I rolled my eyes, realizing he was trying to keep up the suspense, but, hey, at least now I might now get laid out of this deal.

Midmorning the next day, his text arrived. "Meet me at the downtown Macy's at noon today, don't be late. Be ready to satisfy me." This was more like it. Now we were finally getting somewhere. At 11:45 I threw on my coat and headed out of the office toward Macy's. Thinking his choice of meeting spots was a little weird, I shrugged it off, as the entire experience had been a little weird thus far. I spotted him waiting for me just inside the doors of Macy's. Greeting him with a smile, I went to give him a hug. He stopped me, looking at me up and down, and said, "Let's do this." We walked through the store, and I watched him pick up two random shirts from racks and then keep walking. I followed, almost more intrigued of how this was going to play out than caring about the actual event. He then walked into a dressing room and scanned the area for privacy.

Pulling me quickly into the room with him, he finally kissed me. The kiss lacked passion and was more about aggressiveness than romance. He pulled my hair aggressively with one hand, and with the other forcefully grabbed my tit, pinching my nipple until I almost yelped. His assertiveness and control could have possibly been a major turn-on; however, I think I just wasn't 100 percent into him. Continuing on, I wanted to see if it changed and the desire could pick up and get hotter. Right then, it was lukewarm at best.

He whispered to me that I needed to suck his cock. He pushed my head toward his crotch, I undid his pants, watching his cock spring to life. As I leaned in to honor his command, I felt his hand push the back of my head, making me gag on his dick. He then moved his hips hard and fast, plunging into my mouth with a force that was making him more excited with each thrust. Knowing he was approaching his explosion, I pulled back, not wanting to feel or taste him shoot down my throat.

You could sense his aggravation that I didn't swallow or "finish" the job. I was almost amused at the disappointed expression on his face, but I figured he'd get over it. The lack of sexual chemistry partnered with the lack of attraction had come to a head (literally), and I was done. Standing up, I thanked him for the good time, patted him on the shoulder, and said goodbye. Opening the dressing room door, I turned around for one last look. His look of surprise coupled with his pants still around his ankles was priceless.

Chapter 7

"What's a pretty girl like you up to tonight?" A new message appeared in my inbox. I wrote back, "Not much, maybe I was just waiting on you to send me a message." Flirting was fun, and it definitely helped with the ego. Saying whatever you were feeling to a complete stranger, I loved and thrived on how erotic it was. His phone number popped up onto my screen, so I decide to text him. We started talking about the usual—what was I into, had I had any luck on this website, etc. While I was able to emphatically say, "Yes, I have had great luck on this site," he, unfortunately, said that he had yet to meet up with anyone. When I questioned why—as he was a good-looking guy and seemed to be somewhat normal, from what I got from our first conversation—he told me, "That all of the women think I am strange because I don't want to have intercourse with them." Very confused by that answer, as most on this site would be, I asked him to clarify. He said, "I just want to pleasure you. I want to have my way with you, but I don't want anything in return."

Now, this was a bit odd, I am not going to lie, but everyone has their fetish. I actually felt myself feeling a little sorry for the dude and decided that I wanted to throw him a bone. I mean, how bad could it be. I would get pleasure out of the deal. When I told him that I would like to meet up with him, he got a little too excited. Laughing and telling him to calm down, we planned to meet for a drink the next night.

When he walked into the bar, he saw me from a corner table and waved me down. Emphatically wave me down. As I stood up, he hugged me tightly, excited that I had actually shown up. "I told you I would," I said, but he informed me that many women had said they would and that they never did. I had little red flags pop into my head at that moment, but quickly dismissed them, as he seemed a bit goofy but harmless. As we knocked off a few cocktails, we carried on a fairly good conversation. I steered the conversation more toward what may come of the evening, as I was more curious than ever about what he wanted to do to me. Smiling, he suggested we go to a hotel, his treat, and I could find out. A little hesitant, but shrugging it off, I accepted the invitation.

Walking into the motel room (not a hotel), just a block away from the bar, I made a mental note of the door lock, in case I needed to undo it quickly in a bad situation. A girl can never be too sure. He came over to me, brought his hands to my face, and tenderly caressed my cheek. I thought for sure he was going to kiss me, but he didn't, he just whispered in my ear to lie down on the bed. I did, but again, thinking of how I could quickly kick him if he turned out to be a serial killer. Kneeling down between my legs, he proceeded to start to massage my inner thighs. A very slow and very methodical massage. His touch felt amazing, and I started to relax and let myself enjoy the moment.

Massaging closer and closer to my sweet spot, his ability to build a sexual stimulation was off the charts. As he inched closer, I felt myself organically raise my hips in order to try to get closer to his hands, wanting them to touch me. First, I felt one finger slide into me, then two, and then three. With his other hand, he found my clit, and gently rubbed and pinched it between his thumb and forefinger. This touch was not normal, I felt like he had studied this motion in some tantric book. Just as I felt myself wanting to come, he pulled his fingers out of me, and brought them to his mouth. Licking them, he glanced at me, smiling as he knew he left me close to orgasming.

Gently asking me to turn over onto my stomach, he proceeded again to start massaging my inner thighs. By this time I was dripping wet, and I was almost begging to cum. This time, he spread apart my cheeks, and I felt his hot, wet tongue on my ass. I moaned loudly and again felt my hips rise to feel more of his tongue inside me. As I felt his tongue flicker in and out of me, I lost control, cumming uncontrollably. As I came, his lips found their way between my legs, and lapped up every bit of wetness.

As I sat up to get dressed and thank him for an amazing time, I looked up to find him holding my panties to his nose. "What are you doing?" I asked, surprised to see this. "May I have your panties to remember you by?" he asked, continuing to smell my undies. This guy was weird, but I had to give him credit, he definitely knew his way around the female anatomy. I shrugged, thinking this could have ended way worse, so honestly, him wanting to keep my panties really wasn't so bad. "Sure," I said, walking out the door.

Chapter 8

I had been on somewhat of a roll online. My adventures so far had been very self-gratifying, and I was enjoying all the different scenarios that I had been involved in. Everyone, for the most part, had been respectful, pleasant, and satisfying, so I guess I was due to a find a stinker in the mix.

I met IHOP Guy online one day as I took a small break from my workload and logged on to the site from my phone while I was in the office. I had noticed a message from a very good-looking guy, and he seemed extremely charming, catching my attention quickly. I replied to him, sending my phone number, hoping he would text me later. Later turned out to be ten minutes, and his messages quickly started to fill my inbox. He was definitely eager to chat, as I could tell by the plethora of messages, but again, they were all sweet, so I took it in stride.

We traded messages back and forth throughout the evening, sharing minor details of our lives. I found out he was an engineer and worked a lot during the week but spent his weekends hiking in the summer and skiing during the winter months. He was also a bit of a gym rat, hitting the weights about four times a week. If I had been searching for a soul mate, a gym rat would have turned me off immediately. The thought of constantly having to be at the gym, worrying about fattening foods and protein powder, no thank you. But I wasn't searching for my soul mate, I was searching for my next hookup, so I thought I'd just get to have the benefits of running my hands down his washboard abs instead. A win-win.

With all the fitness talk, he surprised me when he chose IHOP as our first meet-up destination. He chose the pancake place on a Thursday night at seven and said he would meet me there. Pulling up to the restaurant, I didn't see him near the entrance, so I went inside. Still not seeing him, I looked at my buzzing phone and saw his text: "I'm already sitting, look in the restaurant." I walked around the corner from the host stand, and I saw his hot face seated at a table, drinking a cup of coffee. He offered a small wave. A bit surprised that he had not been out front to say hello before he sat down, again I pushed the feeling down and joined him. As I sat down, he greeted me with a "Hey" and took another sip of coffee. Then he said, "Catch the waitress when she goes by and tell her what you want." I offered a small grin and flagged her down. When she asked what I was having, I looked at him and asked if he had ordered already. Quickly telling me he was having only coffee, I followed his lead and just ordered a Diet Coke. Once the waitress left us, I turned back toward him. Things had started off a bit odd, but I smiled and asked how he was. We bantered back and forth over our nonalcoholic drinks for the next hour.

An hour later he asked if I was ready to go. I nodded, secretly starving, and hoping this was just a pit stop before we went to a real restaurant, or maybe even that the date was ending and I could go home and eat in the comfort of my home. We headed to the cashier, and she presented the check, totaling $4.32. He quickly corrected the cashier, stating that we would each be paying for our own items. Now, I completely understand that I met this guy on an adult website and my expectations should not be set high, but to go dutch on a bill that was $4.32 blew my mind. Even the cashier had to confirm he was serious. He nodded, completely oblivious to the obvious insanity of the situation. Shaking my head, I pulled out my debit card and handed it to the cashier. She rang up my portion of the bill, then turned toward him. He, too, handed her his card. That's when I heard the obnoxious sound of the credit card machine declining his card. The cashier looked at him, paused, then softly said, "Your card has declined due to insufficient funds. Do you have another method of payment?" I glanced at him expecting to see the embarrassment written on his face, but looking as calm as ever, he just answered, "No."

She looked at me, then him again, then back at me. I think I was more embarrassed than he even remotely was. His card had just declined for $2.50 on the first date! $2.50! Pulling out my debit card once again, I handed it to the cashier, telling her to just put it on my card. She happily obliged, as I think she really just wanted us both to leave. IHOP Guy responded with a thank-you, and proceeded to rub the small of my back as I collected the receipt.

We walked out the door, and immediately I beelined to my car in the parking lot. I couldn't wait for this date to end. I was vaguely aware of him following close behind, but I just kept walking. I was completely shocked this guy wasn't ready to bury his head and run for the hills. Reaching my car, I quickly opened my door and finally turned around to face him. Smiling, he was completely oblivious to everything that had just transpired. Looking at me, he started to lean toward me as if he was going to try to kiss me.

Yes, he was in fact going to try to kiss me, as I noticed his lips had puckered and his eyes began to close. Instinctually, my hand shot up and blocked my face from his. "Are you kidding me?" I stammered. When I saw the look of complete confusion on his face, I knew the best thing to do was just get in my car and leave. As I climbed in my car and threw it in reverse, he continued to just stand there, looking dumbfounded. I shook my head and started laughing at the situation I had just escaped. As I drove home, I swung into the McDonald's drive-through to grab dinner.

Chapter 9

As my time on the website continued, I found myself needing to raise the stakes. I wanted to try some of these new crazy ideas that I had been chatting with strangers about. It was time to dip my toes even deeper into the erotic waters. I had been chatting with a guy for a while that had a big interest in sex parties. Going to them, throwing them, introducing new people to the lifestyle, specifically single women. I knew this most likely wouldn't be a lifestyle that I wanted to live for my whole life, but one time might be a moment that I would remember forever.

Party Guy and I agreed to meet up first so I could ensure he was a "normal" guy with somewhat normal intentions. We met in downtown Seattle for a cocktail one evening after work, and I was pleasantly surprised with his looks, demeanor, and approach, especially with a rookie like me. Party Guy was in his midthirties, sexy, brown wavy hair, and he wore small, round glasses that made him resemble a sexy nerd. He had told me while previously online chatting that he had a serious girlfriend, but that they were in an open relationship, which was also a new term into my vocabulary. It seems that they both enjoyed the party lifestyle, and while committed to each other, they were allowed to comingle with others as well as party together. And by partying together, this meant being at the same party (under the same roof) but able to have sex with others freely. As I mentioned before, this was a whole new life I had entered.

During our conversation, I learned that Party Guy was a civil engineer and worked in the city. He had a very successful career and was able to balance the job and his social life seamlessly. I asked a lot of questions that normally I would have been too shy or hesitant to broach, but his openness and willingness to make me feel comfortable was very inviting. Toward the end of our conversation, he brought up the house party that he was attending that weekend. It was a St. Patrick's Day party, and he knew the attendees intimately and thought this would be the perfect introduction for me, if I was interested. Just in case I worked up the courage to go, I got directions from him as he walked me to my car. As I was about to get in my vehicle, he leaned over and softly kissed me. It was the type of kiss that was soft and alluring but that told me there was so much more where that came from. The kiss immediately turned me on, and I knew at that moment I would be attending the party, if not for the entire atmosphere, but to get more of where this kiss came from.

Friday night arrived, and I was on my way to the party. I was all alone, and the feeling of fear, excitement, and nervousness was almost overwhelming. I entered the quiet neighborhood, wrapping around the winding street until pulling up in front of a beautiful home. The house seemed almost too quiet and too innocent for this type of party, but I had noticed the parade of cars in the driveway telling me that I was at the right place. I quickly reached into my glove box and pulled a bottle of vodka out, bringing the bottle to my lips for a shot of calmness.

Walking up to the door, I double-checked myself in a car door mirror before knocking. The skirt and sweater that I had decided on wearing that evening seemed almost juvenile for a sex party, but that thought caused me to wonder what does one wear to a sex party?

One knock, and the door flew open. I was greeted by two women who had their arms around each other, holding a bottle of whiskey. They immediately threw their arms around me and said they had been expecting me. In I went, with the door closing tightly behind me.

I entered the living room and was excitedly greeted by everyone. There were about fifteen people, both men and women. Everyone was drinking and laughing. Party Guy was in the center of the room, and his face lit up when he saw me walk in. So many of the guests came over to hug and welcome me, I was pleasantly surprised at how warm and welcome I felt in that moment. Party Guy's hug was warm, and he whispered in my ear that I looked amazing and he was glad I had decided to come. My anxiety and fear left in that moment, and the excitement amped up a few notches. As I casually scanned the room, I was keenly aware of another couple in the corner that had not greeted me, as they were too engulfed in each other.

His arms were wrapped around her shirtless back, and they were kissing and grinding in the middle of all the chaos. It was a feeling and a view that was new to me, and I loved it. They were so confident in what they were involved with, not caring at all who was watching. It was a complete turn-on.

The women who had greeted me at the door interrupted my gaze, as they handed me a cocktail, which I happily took. Liquid courage was going to be needed and appreciated tonight! One of the other girls pulled out a stack of what looked like stickers from her pocket and told me about a game that was being played. She told me that they were press-on tattoos, and I was to put it somewhere on my body, and the person who found it would get a prize. I could feel my heartbeat all the way between my legs. This was hot. "What is the prize?" I asked, not really caring, but just making small talk. All the girls just giggled at my question. I took the tattoo and went to the restroom. I remember looking in the mirror, telling myself, "Here goes nothing." I bent down and carefully applied the tattoo on my upper thigh, just before reaching the "promised land." Time to party. I walked back into the living room, wondering how this would get started. Do I have to approach someone and ask if they were interested? Would Party Guy help me get started? Was his girlfriend there, and would she mind? I had those thoughts for a few seconds before the engaging crowd created a circle around me, asking me questions. Was this really my first time at a party like this? What was I into, and was I nervous? I giggled at my previous thoughts and began to enjoy myself. As I was chatting with one of the girls that had given me the tattoo, Party Guy came over to the group. He looked around, apologized to everyone, and said that he had been waiting for me to arrive. In front of everyone, he began kissing me. This wasn't the same sweet kiss he had planted on me at the restaurant; this was a I-want-to-fuck-you-now kiss. His hands glided up and down my body, and his tongue plunged in and out of my mouth. I heard the crowd start to cheer around me before I was completely lost in the moment.

Party Guy then picked me up (literally picked me up) and carried me to a nearby bedroom. We were both ripping the clothes off each other as we climbed into the bed. The kissing continued as I felt my panties being slid off my body. He told me he wanted me since he saw me, and he was going to take it. I hungrily spread my legs apart and pulled him into me. He entered me with such an intensity, all while saying deliciously dirty things, keeping me moaning the entire time. When I finally started to cum, he pulled out of me, and slid down to taste me as I continued to cum in his mouth. It was so satisfying. After orgasming, I was vaguely aware that two guys from the party had come in the bedroom while we had been having sex. They were watching us, and very turned on. One of them, with a thin build with blond hair, looked at us eagerly, asking if he could take a turn. Party Guy looked at me, and I felt myself nodding emphatically. Blond Guy turned me over onto my hands and knees and slid into me. He pumped his rigid cock into me with such force that I had to grab the headboard to steady myself.

He felt wonderful, and I felt my hips bucking along with each thrust. His buddy who had been watching couldn't take being a bystander any longer. I motioned for him to join us (I couldn't believe that I motioned to him), and he climbed onto the bed. He slipped off his shorts, and I immediately took his cock into my mouth. I heard him moan with delight, which made Blond Guy pump me harder. Both guys came at the same time. The feeling of a throbbing cock inside me while having a load shot down my throat was one that I really had no words for. Exhilarating…

I made my way back down to the living room dressed in my skirt and bra. I had left the guys up in the bedroom, as I wanted to continue to explore the party. I sat down on the couch with a new cocktail and started chatting with a group of people that I hadn't seen earlier. As we were talking, a girl came over to me and kneeled down by my legs. She asked if anyone had found my tattoo yet. I shook my head no, as I didn't think I could find my voice, thinking what she was about to do. She then said, "I think I know where it is," with a sly smile that made me instantly want her to find it.

She placed her hands on my knees and slowly pushed my legs apart. As she did this, the entire group of people instantly stopped talking and watched in anticipation. As she pushed my skirt up to the top of my thighs, she whispered that she had found it. She leaned in farther, and I felt her tongue touch me and then enter me. I melted into her mouth. Paired with her warm mouth, I then felt her fingers slide in and out of me. The crowd, now completely turned on, began to kiss each other, and one guy slid my bra off, and my tits found their way to his mouth. The feeling of this erotica partnered with the feeling of being watched was over the top. I began to cum as she licked every inch of me. As she sat up to admire her work, the guy that had been at my tits brought his cock out and slid it into me. As he was in me, I pulled her up to my face, and kissed her passionately, tasting myself on her wet lips. I whispered that I wanted to taste her, and she straddled my face and brought herself down to my waiting lips. It was my first time tasting a woman. She was so soft and tasted so wet and appetizing, I couldn't stop until she was cumming on me. "You got your prize," she whispered breathlessly.

After I gathered my composure, I gathered my clothes and decided it was time to say goodbye to all my newfound friends. Party Guy walked me to the door and mentioned anytime I wanted to see him again or be a party guest, just let him know. We kissed, and off I went. I never did speak with him again, but this was a page in my journey that I would never forget. Personally, I don't even know that every sex party is like the one I was at, and I really don't want to know. I think if I were to experience another sex party, I would never be able to recreate that magic of that night.

Chapter 10

Having been on the website for a few months now, the confidence that I had found within myself spilled into my day-to-day life. Everywhere I went, I felt a renewed sense of calmness and positivity about my life, my body, and my soul. I also found it easier to strike up a conversation with a stranger or carry on a random conversation.

I found it prolific that once you start living your life on your own terms and stop worrying what everyone thinks, it can take a load off the soul.

Every morning on my way to work, I would stop for coffee. Normally I would hit the Starbucks drive-through to dodge the rainy Seattle weather, but with the line becoming increasing longer each day, I decided to try a new spot. Seattle's Best Coffee was also on my way to work, unfortunately it didn't have a drive-through, but I figured I would survive the quick jaunt from my car into the shop.

Running into the coffee shop to get my coffee, I quickly noticed it was very busy and very loud. There was a group of guys that looked as though they were regulars, laughing and drinking their coffees. Also, a couple of local old men were playing cards. I smiled; there is something about the ambiance of a coffee shop that I love. It is so warm and inviting and smells heavenly. My vanilla latte was ready in minutes, and I thanked the barista and made my way back out in the rain to my car. Glancing back at the shop, I noticed a handsome man watching me walk away. When we made eye contact, he waved. I waved back. Wow, how cute is he, I thought. I drove away with a small smile on my face. I immediately wondered if he would be there tomorrow.

Pulling into Seattle's Best the next day, I immediately noticed the cute guy in the same window, same seat as the day before. He noticed me pull up as well and smiled. The butterflies began. I went up to the counter and ordered my vanilla latte. I waited for the coffee, secretly hoping that he might come talk to me. He was sitting among the loud group of guys that were all there the day before, so better to let him come to me than to interrupt the entire group. But nothing happened, and he didn't come talk with me. Bummed, I headed back out to my car, again glancing back at the window. He was still there, looking as cute as ever as he waved again to me. I waved back, climbed into my car, and headed to work.

Day three of Seattle's Best cute guy countdown. I pulled up to the coffee shop, and yes, there he was again. This time, my heart did a little flip-flop. It was once again pouring rain, so I quickly jumped out of the car and dashed into the store. Trying to shake the water off my coat, I checked to see he had noticed that I was there. He was busy talking to the guys, so I headed up to the counter to order my latte. As I pulled out my wallet to pay, the barista told me that my coffee had been paid for already. When I asked by who, a deep voice behind me said, "I took a chance that you would be here again today." I whipped around to find myself face-to-face with the cute coffee guy from the window. Smiling, and his eyes twinkling with a bit of mischief, he gestured to a small table nearby and asked if he could steal a moment of my time. Of course I wanted to yell, Who cares about work! But I politely answered with a simple "Yes."

We chatted for a bit over our morning coffee, and I found myself smitten with him. I found out he was a painter (houses, not artwork), and that he and his father, together, have their own business. The guys I saw him with each day all worked for him, and they all stopped here for breakfast each day before starting work. He said he had noticed me come in and thought I was cute. I told him I thought the same thing and was hoping that he would come talk with me.

About twenty minutes into the conversation, his friends caught on that he had slipped away and was sitting with me. They came over to introduce themselves and razz him a bit, trying to embarrass him. This was my cue to leave and head to work. Walking me to my car he asked if I would like to have dinner with him that weekend. Yes!

We met at a Mexican restaurant that was somewhere between both of our houses. He greeted me in the parking lot with a warm hug and a kiss on my cheek and held my hand as we headed inside. We grabbed a booth, ordered a couple of cocktails, and for the next hour I found myself lost in good conversation, his eyes, and his dazzling smile. After dinner, I think he read my mind, asking me to join him at his place for a beer. I followed his car for the five-minute trip to his house, thinking the whole time what it would feel like to be in his arms.

We got to his place, a charming little house just on the outskirts of Seattle. Decorated modestly, a clean bachelor pad was my first thought. As soon as I walked in, I didn't have to wait long to find out about that feeling. He took me in his arms and kissed me deeply. He whispered, "I've been wanting to do that for a while now, and it's just as good as I imagined it." We kissed awhile more, and decided it was a great night to put on a movie and cuddle in front of the fireplace. A little more of a romantic feel than I had been experiencing lately, but it was welcomed and wanted. While he tended to the fireplace, I selected a movie, which at this point in time, I could not even tell you what we watched because I don't think we saw any of it. Once the fire came to life, he spread a blanket in front of it and patted the open area next to him, motioning me to join him. I was wrapped up in his arms again immediately. Painter Guy slowly undressed me while kissing every inch of my body.

Between each kiss he would make eye contact with me, and his look drove me crazy. I trembled with excitement, wanting that feeling to last all night. He stood up and undressed, allowing me to watch his every move. You could tell he was more turned on by my eyes glued to his body. By the firelight, he was a vision with his tattoos and muscles. He slid off his pants and watched me gasp at the size of him. He was by far my biggest yet, and I couldn't wait to test the theory if size really matters.

He lay down, pulling me close. Kissing me on my ears and neck heated up the moment (not that it needed more heat) even more so, and when he softly entered me, I was more than ready. I inhaled at the size and shock of how good he felt, and moved my hips along with his thrusts. He was gentle and rough all in the same moment. The chemistry that we felt throughout the entire act was electric.

Painter Guy and I had more going on than my past hookups. There was a connection that happened organically, and if I allowed myself to, I could have found myself falling for him. He was sweet and romantic, thoughtful, and kind. His actions in and outside of the bedroom were amazing and commendable. Flowers were delivered to my work, long conversations were had, and overnights were consistent. On the flip side, I spent many evenings arguing with my heart about letting myself fall for him. We were definitely building something substantial, and it scared me. I knew I wasn't ready for a relationship.

Painter Guy was taking me on a picnic one beautiful weekend day when he mentioned we needed to stop by his parents' house to pick something up. My head started spinning at the thought of meeting his parents. I didn't believe that I was ready for this step, but I went along with him to make the most of the situation. Upon arriving at their house, I met his mother and father, both hugging me and making me feel warm and welcome in their home. With smiles on their faces, they began to tell me of their excitement of their son finally finding *the one.* Secretly panicking, I immediately felt guilty, knowing that I was not planning the same future with their son that they had in mind. I hugged them one last time before we left.

On our drive to the picnic, I knew what I needed to do. I needed to tell Painter Guy that I was not prepared for a relationship; I had been divorced for only six months, and I clearly wasn't ready to jump into another serious relationship so soon. Nervously thinking on how to begin, he spoke first, and confessed that he had fallen in love with me. He wanted to build a life together with me and my daughter (he had not met my daughter yet), but he was sure I was the one.

Asking him to pull over, I looked at his eager expression as he waited to hear if I would now confess my love for him. I felt tears stream down my face as I told him that we couldn't continue our relationship. That I was not ready—mentally or physically—for a serious partner in my life. I hated myself in the moment, but I knew I was doing the right thing. I had to tell him how I felt before this went any further. Looking crushed and sad, he told me he understood, but he had hoped I would feel differently about him. I asked him to take me home; I felt it was best we end it now instead of continuing with our date. He nodded. We drove to my house in an awkward, sad silence. When we arrived, I turned to him, hugging him, apologizing again. He kissed my cheek and said, "When you decide you are ready, look me up and I might still be single." Giving a small grin, I nodded and closed the car door behind me.

Chapter 11

Coming close to being in a relationship and then ending it can leave one feeling a little bruised. I spent the next few weeks just being a mom and a career woman. I stayed away from the computer, from the website, allowing my mind and soul to focus on what steps were next for me.

About a month later, feeling much better, I ventured back on to the site, seeing my email overflowing with men asking and waiting for my reply. As I began the familiar process of deleting the requests with the usual pickup lines, I received a ping alerting me to a guy who was looking to start a conversation. His opening line was "I am the best ever at going down on woman, I will make you scream like you never have before." I rolled my eyes and deleted the conversation. Too cocky for me. Another ping, and his name popped up again. "Don't you want me to prove it to you?" I deleted it again. A third ping. "Why won't you respond to me, don't you think I'm adorable?" Responding, I questioned, "Why are you so persistent?" "Because you are beautiful, and I want to meet you." Good answer, I thought.

I messaged him my phone number, and we immediately began chatting. Nothing about this guy was my type, but he really was adorable, so I made an exception. He was much younger than me, having just turned twenty-three years old. During our conversation, I told him I couldn't believe I was talking to someone so young. He was just a baby in my eyes, what could he possibly want with me? But he loved the attention, and mentioned that he loved older women. He told me to teach him a thing or two. I laughed. If he only knew of my sexual adventure that I had embarked on. I found out he was an Army Ranger, stationed at Fort Lewis, just forty-five minutes from where I lived. Oh, how I love a man in uniform.

After chatting for a couple of weeks, I knew I was ready to get back on the horse (so to speak) and meet Ranger Boy. We met up that next weekend at a casual burger restaurant not too far from my house. I saw him standing outside the restaurant waiting for me to arrive. Trotting over to my car immediately, he even opened the door for me. He was a vision of handsomeness, much cuter than his pictures were online. He had strawberry-blond hair, short, in a military-style haircut, his build was strong and sturdy. He had a large dimple on each cheek, making me want to kiss them emphatically.

He engulfed me into a hug that was more crushing than romantic, making me yelp, causing us both to laugh, breaking the ice. Heading into the restaurant he grabbed my hand in his, which was both inviting and a sweet gesture. Inside, we had great conversation paired with a couple cocktails. We were having a great time. After about an hour, I felt his hand brush my leg under the table. He looked at me with such sex appeal and intensity, and whispered in a throaty voice, "Let's get out of here."

He followed me to my car, and for the first time I noticed the helmet in his hands. He rode a bike, which immediately made him ten times hotter. I smiled at the thought of him straddled on that crotch rocket, his hair blowing in the wind, looking ever so sexy. When he asked if he could hop in my passenger seat, I gladly waved him in. The doors hadn't even closed yet before we were locked in a heated embrace. Taking a pause from kissing, he suggested we hop into the back seat. Laughing, we both changed seats, not even caring to notice if people had seen us. In the back seat, his hand slid into my jeans, and his fingers found their way quickly inside me, sliding in easily with how excited I was. I began to moan and move with his hands, pausing for a moment, while he brought his hands to his mouth and tasted me.

I was wild to get his pants undone and get him inside me. He didn't resist as I pulled the buttons apart on his Levi's. Soon we were moving together, his cock slowly sliding in and out of me. He came quickly, yet was still hard as a rock and still ready for more. Oh, to be twenty-three again.

Ranger Boy continued to blow up my phone over the next couple of weeks. We saw each other almost every other day, whether it was to grab a bite to eat or to get it on in the back seat of my car. Finally, after a few weeks, I found myself in his bed, able to spend the entire evening with him. More comfortable than my car, although not much sleeping got accomplished. While I was able to teach the boy a few things about technique, his stamina was off the charts. He continues to hold my record of having sex nine times in one night.

He confided in me that I was the first woman to give him a blow job to completion and finish the job. His mind, as well as his dick, were blown. After that inaugural BJ, that was a must-do for every encounter moving forward.

Ranger Boy wanted to get serious. He asked many times to be committed to each other, as he was desperate for a relationship. While I enjoyed every minute with him, the age difference was too great, and I almost felt silly for dating a guy so much younger than me. After about a month of seeing each other, I decided to end the relationship. He continued to text me, checking back to see if I had changed my mind. Tragically, two weeks later I found out that my hot Ranger Boy had passed away. He had been driving his motorcycle late at night going over a hundred miles an hour when he collided with another car head-on and lost his life. I will always remember his sweet dimples and his everlasting evenings.

Chapter 12

I hadn't even read his email that he sent to me; I just couldn't get past his profile picture. Clicking on the picture to enlarge it and take a closer look, I saw one of the sexiest men that I had ever laid eyes on. His piercing green eyes seem to jump off the screen, looking right into my most intimate thoughts. He wore a tan flannel shirt that hugged his muscles and blue jeans that appeared to be a second skin on his body. A cowboy hat and a chiseled jawline completed the look. Finally tearing my gaze away from his picture, I clicked into his email that he had sent. "Saddle up, my sweet little cowgirl, let's go for a ride." I squealed with delight right there in my living room, as I thought not only do I get to sleep with this guy and run my hands all over that body of his, but the fact that he sounded and looked like a cowboy was an immediate turn-on. I wanted to roll in the hay with him.

Having been super excited to chat with him, I was a little disappointed once we actually started to banter. He seemed very shy in both texts and on the phone, almost awkward at times. He struggled to keep the conversation consistently going, causing long pauses in the dialogue, which I started to grow bored with. To keep myself not only awake, but stimulated and wanting to proceed with the conversation, I kept looking at his picture, remembering the face and the body on the other end of the call. All the while I was wondering, how could someone so hot be so damn boring? Maybe he just wasn't a phone guy. Maybe the chemistry would be off the charts when I met him in person. Interrupting his monotone conversation, I blurted out that we should just stop talking and meet.

I had suggested a movie for our first outing, my motive being he didn't have to talk much, and I could just secretly gaze at his beauty. Terrible thought, I know, but it was better than hearing him ramble about nothing important. We had decided to meet at the theater, and walking in I spotted him in the popcorn line. Instantly disappointed, he looked a lot less handsome than he had been in his picture. He had put on some pounds since that picture had been taken, and his hair was longer, almost taking on a mullet-type look. His face and smile were still enough to melt me, but I found it interesting that he had changed so much since his picture. I couldn't help thinking that I would think that you'd want someone to think you were better looking in person, but I guess he felt differently. After all, I was here on the date because of that picture, where I may not have been if there was a current picture. Online dating is so superficial. We judge and are judged first by the way we look.

Deciding to still go all in, I snuck up behind him in line, and I slid my arms around his waist. Startled, he jumped, spilling his soda all over the counter. Turning bright red, he grinned at me, embarrassed by the moment. I laughed, and although the romantic moment had been killed, the ice had been broken, literally.

The theater was already dark and showing previews when we made our way in, and once my eyes adjusted to the darkness I realized that all the seats were empty. Must not be a popular movie, I thought. Selecting two seats in the middle of the theater, my mind started to race, wondering what naughty things we could do in a movie theater that we have all to ourselves. As the main movie started to roll, there still was not a person in sight. I felt my heart racing as I looked over at Cowboy. The thought of doing it in such a public place had me already wet. Innocently, Cowboy was staring intently at the movie, not having an idea what kind of dirty thoughts were brewing next to him.

My hand slowly reached over to Cowboy's thigh and ran it along his leg until it came to a stop, resting on the outline of his cock. His head snapped sideways to look at me, and I knew the moment was on. Continuing to rub my hand over the now bulge in his pants, I heard his breathing quicken. I giggled when I finally saw him glance around the theater and realize that we were alone. I thought, He's a little late to the party, but better late than never. Leaning over, I unzipped his jeans and took his cock out. It was a beautiful cock, about nine inches in length with a girth worth bragging about. As I slowly started to run my hands up and down the shaft, I brought my mouth to it. Taking in the entire cock, I felt myself almost gag on it as it touched the back of my throat. I heard him quietly moan and saw him grip the arms of the seat tighter. I let my head drop a little lower, grabbing his balls in my mouth, lightly sucking one and then the other. When he would start to squirm in his seat, I would go back to his cock, running my tongue up and down it.

He grabbed my hair and pushed my face farther down onto his cock. "I'm going to cum," he whispered. I nodded with my mouth still wrapped around him and waited for the explosion. Once he came, I think he thought we were done, but I wasn't even close to stopping. I was just getting started. Turning around in my seat and grabbing the back of my chair, I motioned for him to enter me. Pushing my ass out, I wanted to feel that big cock in me. Looking around again, I could tell he was nervous. Leaning over again, I pressed my lips to his, feeling every corner of his mouth with my tongue. Then I whispered in his ear, "Do you want to fuck me?" He nodded, jumped up, and grabbed my hips and thrust his cock into me. We both groaned with immense pleasure. Continuing to pump in me, his fingers slid down from my hips and found my ass. As he slid a finger into my tight hole, he continued to thrust his cock as hard as he could. In pure bliss, I could feel every thrust, and I never wanted it to stop. I felt my orgasm coming quickly, and I couldn't contain my moaning. I am sure I was louder than I meant to be, but no one was there to hear me. And if they did, well, maybe they would have found themselves turned on as well.

Sitting back down, Cowboy pulled me over to him. I heard him whisper, "Ride my cock, reverse cowgirl. It's my favorite." Silently questioning if this was why he thought of himself as a cowboy, I straddled his cock, with my back to him. It was a little tricky to maneuver this position in the movie theater seats, but we actually managed quite well, and I found it incredibly satisfying. Holding his ankles, I grinded myself against him, rubbing my clit just in the right spot. His hands again started to explore my ass, finding their way back into my tight hole. That must be his thing, I thought.

Completely lost in the moment, I hadn't realized that the theater usher had come in to check on things in the theater. As the flashlight beam landed directly on my face, I froze in mid-thrust, as did Cowboy. "What are you two doing?" he questioned. The usher couldn't have been more than sixteen years old, and looked completely terrified at what he had just encountered. I almost laughed out loud, but I held it in and yelled back, "Nothing."

We were busted!

"Get your things, and I am going to have to ask you to leave," he said timidly. And with that comment, he headed out of the theater. Laughter erupted from both of us, and I scrambled off him and quickly got dressed. As we walked out of the theater, pretending to hold our heads down in shame, the usher was waiting, with his hands on his hips. "You need to leave," he said as he motioned toward the door.

Still laughing when we got into the car, Cowboy shook his head and said he couldn't believe we had done that. "Want to grab a drink after that fiasco?" he asked. Just around the corner we found a cute little dive bar, grabbed a couple of barstools and a couple of beers. Looking closer at him, now that we were in the light, I could still see a lot of the handsome, sexy features that had been in his original profile picture. Those piercing green eyes were still mesmerizing, and that chiseled jaw, well, it had given way to a little more weight, but it could still be seen, just not as pronounced as before. Grabbing his hands across the table, I was still reeling in the magic from the theater.

Sadly, the same awkward banter that occurred over the phone showed itself in person as well. While I was completely comfortable and eager to talk about what just happened, he became quiet and shy. I tried to keep the conversation going, even asking him about his cowboy hat in his profile picture, asking where he was from and if he was a true cowboy. Blushing, he shook his head. "I found that the hat and the pickup line works really well on women. I'm not a cowboy. I'm originally from California. My favorite position is reverse cowgirl, and that is where I got the idea." Well, I had to give the guy credit for creating a sexy persona. If he had gone into the dating site with no pickup line, no hat, and a current picture, I don't think that I would have even noticed him or texted him back. But here he was, sitting with me, getting laid in the movie theater. Overall, the evening was one for the books, but not worthy of a second chapter.

Chapter 13

If nothing else, on a quiet evening when my daughter was with her father, online chatting definitely kept me entertained. It took the place of any crap TV show I would have watched. And talk about real reality TV, I had my own drama going on right from my own computer!

Being in the online chat rooms within the website, it was almost tough to keep a conversation straight, as I was interrupted with so many others chiming in to try to chat with me as well. After a few opening lines, I now had a good idea if they would be able to keep my attention for a few minutes, so, as usual, that helped weed out a lot of the candidates. As I was chatting with one guy, I was only about 50 percent vested in our ongoing conversation. He was okay to talk with, but nothing that had me intrigued. That is until he mentioned he was a police officer. As I mentioned in the previous chapter, I love a man in uniform, and even better if that uniform gave them some power. Deleting all the other windows that had open conversations, I was now all in with Policeman. He was on the force for a suburb of Seattle for the last ten years. As we continued to chat, he texted me a few pictures of himself, one of himself in uniform, aviator sunglasses on, and I was officially smitten.

We agreed to meet up, just to say hello and have a cup of coffee before taking things to the next level. His idea was to test the chemistry and ensure we both wanted to move forward. We scheduled a coffee date for midmorning the next day.

Arriving at the cafe a little early, I ordered my latte and grabbed a table near the window of the parking lot. This way, I could watch him pull up and prepare myself before he walked in. A few minutes later, I saw a squad car pull up, and Policeman hopped out of the car. He was in full uniform (YES!), and he was more handsome in person than in his photos. Probably about five ten, stocky build, and his dark-brown hair was cut short. Walking in, he scanned the room until his eyes locked on mine. Smiling at me, he gestured that he'd be over after he ordered his coffee, and I nodded.

Trotting over to me, coffee in hand, he held his arms out to welcome me into a hug. I gladly accepted and found myself engulfed in a powerful bear hug. We sat down, smiling and both agreeing that we were pleasantly happy with the meet and greet thus far. While getting to know each other, our conversation had to work around the constant chatter on his radio. Not minding at all, I was quite turned on by the whole package—the face, the personality, the uniform, the gun, etc. All of him was just sexy and powerful, and I wanted to be his "bad girl."

Finally, a call came across that he couldn't ignore. He apologized, as he was on duty and had to run. We both stood up, hugging once again, and I realized he smelled so good. Musky with a small hint of aftershave. I waved goodbye as he jumped in his car and sped off. Gulping the rest of my coffee, I smiled to myself at the thought of ripping that uniform off him, and hoping to know what that was like sooner rather than later.

I didn't have to wait long at all to have that feeling come to life. On my way home, Policeman texted me. "It was so good to meet you. Let's have dinner tonight, I will cook for you. Meet me at my place at 7." Squealing with delight, I texted back, "Sure thing. See you tonight." Trying to decide what to wear, I settled on a casual dress with a cardigan. I didn't want to appear overdressed, especially when we were staying home, but I wanted to look like I took some time trying to look my best.

The door swung open to his home, and Policeman greeted me with the same warm hug as earlier, but this time he added a kiss. His kiss was everything I had imagined, soft but assertive, protective but sexual. I found myself whispering, "Can dinner wait awhile?" He smiled, nodded, and led me to his bedroom. Scooping me off the ground and laying me gently on the bed, he kissed me again, and said, "Make yourself comfortable, I will be right back." He disappeared down the hall, and I wasted no time undressing and climbing under the warm covers on his bed.

Moments later, he walked back into the bedroom in full uniform (minus the gun) and told me to get up. Hurrying to my feet, he gently pushed my naked body against the wall, and whispered into my ear, "You have the right to remain silent, and anything you do will be held against you." My heart was pounding, I was so turned on it was hard to concentrate. I could feel the warmth of his breath on my neck and ear, while I felt his cock pressing against me through his pants. Hearing a clicking noise, I quickly felt the cold metal of handcuffs clasp around my wrists. I moaned with delight, loving every minute.

Still standing against the wall, I heard him unzip his pants, waiting patiently for him to drive that cock inside me. Without warning, he was inside me, pumping hard and fast, so much so that I had to lean heavily on the wall to keep my balance. With my hands restrained behind my back, I loved being at his mercy. This had been the control I was searching for! Finally turning me around, coming face-to-face, he picked me up and tossed me onto the bed. Straddling my face, he eased his cock into my mouth and gently began moving his hips. I sucked and licked his cock like a lollipop until I could feel he was ready to cum. He pulled out of my mouth just before exploding and shot his load between my tits.

Now without the handcuffs, I finally was able to wrap my arms around him. He kissed me softly, running his hands up and down my body. I began to peel off his uniform, wanting to feel his naked body against mine. Entwined in each other, we drifted off to sleep.

The rest of the evening with Policeman was sensual and erotic. He had pulled out all the stops for a romantic dinner. We ate in his living room, on the floor, naked on a blanket, picnic style. The menu was an array of finger foods, so needless to say we did a lot of feeding each other. Eating is so much more stimulating when you are eating it off of your partner. Some of the food, especially dessert, found its way onto more erotic body parts. Drizzling chocolate sauce on each other's bodies and licking it off was tantalizing and incredibly hot.

As I kissed him good night, he touched my face, looking deep into my eyes. "Please tell me this doesn't end here." I had no words for him. If I had not been recently divorced, and still healing, he would be a wonderful guy to possibly explore the future with. But knowing that my heart wasn't fully healed yet, tearfully saying, "I'm sorry," I gave him one last kiss and left.

Chapter 14

My life had been going really well. My daughter was doing great in school, my job was flourishing and keeping me busy, and my love life, well, my sex life was quite exhilarating and satisfying. Online dating was oddly easy, and having sex with strangers was more gratifying than I had ever dreamed. The ability to quench my sexual desires and live out my fantasies without commitment was better than I had imagined. Surely, things couldn't always be this smooth.

Getting ready for work one morning, I knew I had a site appointment with a local law firm that needed to possibly use my hotel meeting space for their local meeting. The business was needed, so I took special pains that morning getting dressed in my lucky business suit and taking a little extra time to get ready. Five minutes before the meeting was scheduled to take place, I took my place in the lobby of my hotel, ready to greet my guests. The group arrived together, all gentlemen, bundled up from the rain and wind outside. Exchanging introductions, I began my usual sales pitch of what we had to offer for their upcoming event. As I toured the group throughout the hotel, I noticed one gentleman lingering back closer to me as the others continued to walk ahead and look at the meeting space.

Once the rest of the group was out of earshot, the lingering man finally glanced over at me and apologized for staring. Then blurted out, “I know it’s you from the website. I was on the site last night trying to get you to notice me. This is amazing that I get to meet you here, like this.” In shock, and trying to think of what to say, I immediately walked away from him, and quickly walked ahead to catch up with the rest of the group.

Remembering I had worried about this happening in the beginning of my adventure, I had gotten so comfortable on the website, that I had dismissed the feeling after a handful of successful dates. Now, feeling the heat and embarrassment creep into my face, I tried the best I could to regroup and find my place. Finding my professional voice, I described the room that we were currently standing in and offered up the benefits it had, benefits that would be suitable for their event. As we continued the tour, I answered their questions and faked a level of interest and enthusiasm, all the while secretly yearning for this site tour to end. Avoiding eye contact with “the guy,” I was able to make it through, although at one point I glanced in his direction, and he was still smiling with such enthusiasm that I thought I would throw up.

Somehow, professionally, I managed to complete the tour. As I was saying goodbye to the group of gentlemen, I shook their hands, having to shake “his” hand as well. As our hands touched, he mouthed the words "call me" and headed out into the rain with his coworkers. Turning toward my office, I couldn't wait to be behind a closed door, where I continued to try to gather myself. Reliving the moment in my head, I realized he had seen my picture on the adult website and then recognized me in my safe place, my place of work. A place that was not allowed to collide with my new personal life I had created. Able to comfortably handle both lives separately, I was not prepared to handle, nor did I want to, handle them together. I had to stop this before it happened again.

After logging on to my computer that evening, I pulled up the website. Immediately noticing more email requests than usual, I quickly realized that all of the requests were coming from one person: my new "friend." I had over twenty messages from him, most of them with relatively the same message, "What are the chances that we met today? It's fate. I just wanted to rip your clothes off. I could tell you felt the same. Call me. Here's my number." The excitement he wrote with was off the charts, almost causing me to laugh. The guy clearly could not read signs, as I had been repulsed and embarrassed by the situation, a far cry from being turned on.

Seeing that I was now online, he sent multiple online requests to chat. "I want to see you tonight, are you available? Please I need to see you."

The desperate and endless messages to try to get my attention were definitely not helping his situation. I pondered the best way to tell him that this was never going to happen. I never wanted to even see him again, nor did I want to continue our communication. I went with the direct approach. "This is never going to happen. My work life and my personal life cannot overlap." I kept typing. "I am sorry to be an ass, but thanks but no thanks." At that point, I deleted all his chats, feeling that he should get the message with my response. I clicked my computer off and headed to bed.

The next morning, before work, I logged back on to the site. He had left me a message with a sad emoji face but nothing else. I think he understood my message. Breathing a sigh of relief, I was relieved but now troubled that this situation may happen again. Clearly, I had been wrong about the type of people who were on this website, and now I was hesitant to continue. Naively I had assumed that the class of people that I worked with were completely different than the class of people that were on the site. But I was on the site...and the lawyer had been on the site. Apparently I wasn't the only "normal" person trying to live out my fantasies.

Looking at my profile picture, I wondered what would happen if I just deleted the photo. The way I looked at the situation, it was just way too risky to keep it. This situation was bound to find me again, and I might not be able to navigate through it so quickly or gracefully the next time. Clicking the delete button, I sadly wondered if this would put an end to my exotic ride. It was a ride that I was not ready to get off yet; I felt as though I was just finding my stride in this journey. It was just a ride, however, and if I was comparing my "ride" with my career, there was no comparison. I had worked my whole life to establish my reputation and build my career, and was not about to jeopardize that to sow some wild oats.

Chapter 15

Turns out not having a picture on the website wasn't going to slow my journey down; I still had offers pouring in to meet up. As I had mentioned before, the website is made of up a majority of single men looking to get laid, so having a picture or not, if they see you are a female looking for a good time, they are going to give it a try. Pussy is pussy, I guess.

Without the picture, I felt more protected and in control of the situation. I was able to now determine who gets to see my picture versus it just being out there for everyone to see. It was another way to preserve my privacy, until I was ready to move to the next level with someone. Feeling satisfied with my new decision, browsing through the new emails and profile pictures, I poured myself a glass of wine and settled in to find my next thrill.

In my list of new emails, I found one that stuck out from the rest, probably because it was a face picture instead of another dick pic. The guy in the picture was posing with his shirt off, wearing blue jeans with his baseball hat on backward. Baseball hats were my weakness, and if they were backward, good lord, you could almost guarantee you were going to get laid. He had sent an email the day prior, with a tagline "batter up." The tagline alone intrigued me, and I emailed him back, "I'm on deck, and dying to be in the game," thinking I would be cute and continue this baseball theme.

Quickly I received an online chat from him asking for my phone number. Sharing it, I heard the familiar ping of my phone and saw the text, "Hey, it's me, game on." Smiling, I texted back and felt the familiar hunger and desire start to creep up. I learned that Baseball Guy was in real life a baseball player (not just his persona); he was on the Triple-A baseball team for the Yankees. Whoa! The Yankees! The baseball theme now made so much more sense, and his "hot" meter just increased immensely! We continued the baseball theme until it was so far overdone and just silly; from balls to bats, we used every dirty related joke imaginable. It was corny, but it did the trick. Both of us were turned on and eager to meet up. We agreed to meet up after work the next day for a cocktail.

Walking in and scanning the bar, I realized I had beat him there. I preferred it that way, knowing I could have a cocktail and get comfortable. Walking in and trying to scan the room for a face that you have only seen in one picture online can be a little intimidating. Especially if they are already there and watching you. Ordering my cocktail, I settled into a nearby barstool and waited for Baseball Guy.

I spotted the backward New York Yankees cap instantly. I smiled, and he sidled up next to me at the bar. Putting his arm around me, he extended his other hand and introduced himself. He was as cute as his picture, even cuter, really. Perfect teeth, great smile, tall, like six two maybe, and lean but muscular build. The confidence that he immediately exuded was apparent and was a complete turn-on. He ordered a beer, winked at me, and motioned to a nearby table that was in a quieter location. He whispered in my ear that he needed to tell me what he wanted to do to me. Then I felt the tip of tongue graze the inside curve of ear. Holy shit, I needed this guy.

Moving to the quieter table, he sat down on the same side as me and scooted his chair closer until we were almost touching. I had worn a skirt that day, and it wasn't five minutes into our conversation before I felt his hand on my bare thigh. Again, looking at him, he gave me that charming grin and wink, and continued to slide his hand upward until it completely disappeared under my skirt. Mid-sentence, I felt his fingers slip into me, going in and out, rubbing and exploring. Losing my train of thought, I felt my body grind against his fingers, vaguely aware that we were still in public. He pulled his hand back up and licked his fingers. I felt my knees go weak. "Let's get out of here," he said.

The walk to the car felt like miles. I just wanted to feel him against me, and inside me. When I went to climb into the back seat, he stopped me, pointing to the front seat. He got into the driver's seat, and then pulled me down into his lap, straddling him. Pulling his cock out, I couldn't help but notice how large it was. I quickly sat on top of it, letting it slide into me, filling up every inch of me. He moved me up and down, sideways, and fast and slow on that cock. He knew what he was doing, and I was enjoying every minute.

Going home that evening, I thought of Baseball Guy. He was an amazing time, and I was interested in hitting that one again. I didn't hear from him until later that week. Randomly one morning I received a text from him asking me to meet him for lunch. At his place. I smiled and secretly placed a bet with myself that we were not going to be eating any food. I texted him yes, asked him for the address, and jumped in my car.

I pulled up to a small house in the seedy part of Seattle. I saw his car in the driveway, confirming I was at the right place. There was another car in the driveway as well, but not thinking anything of it, I headed to the door. I knocked and heard his familiar voice yelling, "Come in." I opened the door, immediately seeing Baseball Guy on his couch, backward hat still on, but nothing else. His cock was already at attention and ready to work. He gave me that adorable grin and told me to get naked and wrap my mouth around his cock. Shedding my clothes probably faster than I ever have, I dropped to my knees, grabbing him in my mouth. It was at that point I heard another voice come from the bedroom, a man's deep voice. "Is she here yet?" I stopped sucking and looked up at Baseball Guy. He gave me that wink. "I told my buddy what a good fuck you were, and he wanted to see for himself. I hope that's okay."

I had started this sexual quest for exploration and fulfilling fantasies that I had only ever read about. Now, organically I had stumbled into one of these situations that you can't make up even if you tried. Nodding to Baseball Guy that I was ready for what was to come, I went back to sucking his cock as he started to moan. I looked up, with my mouth still on Baseball Guy to see his buddy coming out of the bedroom. His friend, looking amused and turned on, came over to watch me blow his buddy. Taking a seat next to us on the couch, and not taking his eyes off me, he slid his shorts down to his ankles, revealing his wide-awake cock. With Baseball Guy and his buddy sitting next to me, I slid sideways and grabbed his friend's cock in my mouth. I caught Baseball Guy's approving look as I sucked his buddy. For the next few minutes, I played the "switch hitter," alternating cocks in my mouth. It was exhausting and exhilarating at the same time. Both cocks were satisfyingly large, filling up my mouth each time I wrapped my lips around them.

As I moved from Baseball Guy to his buddy's cock, Baseball Guy stood up and got behind me. I felt his cock against my ass and then enter me. Moaning, I sucked his buddy harder as he pummeled me from behind. I felt his buddy push his cock deeper into my mouth, moaning louder, and I knew he was going to cum. I happily took the load, as I felt Baseball Guy pump me harder, getting turned on from what was transpiring in my mouth. His buddy, now lying on the couch, motioned for me to climb on top of him. Ready to change positions, I straddled him, feeling his hands on my tits, and feeling Baseball

Guy's eyes on us. I was so turned on by everything happening, I felt myself cumming harder than normal. I collapsed in a heap on his buddy's chest. My gamble had been right. I hadn't been there to eat lunch, and I was completely okay with that.

Chapter 16

For the most part of my sexual journey, my encounters thus far continued to be satisfying. This was a little by luck, but also the fact that I took my time while chatting and actually tried to get to know these men before meeting them. I weeded through hundreds of chats, emails, and texts before deciding that someone sounded sane enough to take a chance on. My deal-breakers were simple, I thought. Never was anyone ever allowed to meet my daughter, and usually they didn't even know about her. It wasn't something I frequently shared in conversations. Knowing where I lived was also never an option. When living alone with a four-year-old, I would never take the chance of giving out my address. If ever the topic of being a single mother did come up in a conversation, I was blown away by the number of people that said, "Just put your daughter to bed and let me come over." I learned quickly that people are sick. Not only did I never speak to those people again, but I blocked them within the website. First and foremost, my daughter and her needs always came first. This sexual expedition that I was on was something for me and was only done when my daughter was in the safety of her dad's care.

Again, as I mentioned above, most of the adventures I had embarked on thus far were memory-worthy; however, there were still many that were not worth writing an entire chapter about. Those that had gotten a first date, but the journey ended there. In this part of the adventure, in my head I always imagine this is where the training montage with the big hit song in the *Rocky* movies would play. A montage of bad first dates, with me looking disgusted or maybe amused, and then shaking my head as they lean in for a kiss at the end of the date.

Throughout this process, I continued to learn more about myself every day. From the good dates to the bad dates, each one taught me a new lesson and helped me increase my awareness of what I needed in my life to be truly happy. To be the person that I am supposed to be. At the end of this exploration, whenever that may be, I wanted to be able to look back and not regret anything, to realize that I took chances and came out a better person because of it. To have jumped onto this wild ride knowing that there would be times of fear and times where I felt fearless.

I was not yet at the end of my adventure, just reflecting on what had already transpired and what was to come. The most important thing was that I enjoyed finding out what made me happy, what made me satisfied.

One night, after a few glasses of wine, I was feeling a little more spicy than usual. Logging on to the website in that type of mood might seem dangerous to some, but to me it allowed me the courage I needed to try something new. Another notch on my sexual exploration journey. Logging in, I decided to change things up a bit. I switched from my usual search of single men to couples looking to add a third to the mix. The more the merrier, right?

Just as I had found there was a plethora of single men looking for hookups, there was also a sizable market for couples that were in search of some fun. I "flirted" with a few good-looking couples by sending them a "flirt" emoji, and waited to see if anything would come of it. Within fifteen minutes, I had received emails from five of the couples I had clicked on earlier. Knowing I had to whittle it down from there, I started emailing all of them, hoping to be able to pare down the options as I got to know them.

An hour later, my favorite couple and I were still emailing, so I decided to share my phone number and continue the conversation from there. Being honest and up-front with them, I let them know that I was a single female, and this would be my first experience with a couple. Being unaware of the new rules, assuming that they must be somewhat different than a normal hookup, I quickly learned I would be entering into a much more intimate and delicate situation. I wanted to ensure that I was respectful and didn't cross any boundaries that had been set by the couple. As I continued to text with them, my sexual anticipation grew, knowing that I wanted to give this a try. Being honest with myself, I fully embrace that I am a heterosexual woman, but that being said, I think women's bodies are beautiful and sexy. Soft, supple, and usually curvy, the thought of getting to be with both a man and a woman at the same time was a bit mind blowing.

Driving to Tacoma, which was about forty-five minutes from Seattle, I spent the drive psyching myself up for what was about to happen. Not only was I about to embark on a new sexual experience, I was meeting them at their home for the first encounter. Normally I played it very safe and first met the person at a public place. However, somehow in my mind I had processed this situation into thinking it must be safe, as there was another female involved.

I pulled up to a cute little house in a normal-looking neighborhood. Breathing a small sigh of relief, I approached the door with a burning curiosity of what I would find on the other side. A very normal-looking couple answered the door together, ready to welcome me and trying to put me instantly at ease. They almost looked more nervous than me, later confessing that they had tried to make this work so many times, but every time they got close to setting this situation up, something didn't work out. Most of the time, the "other" woman didn't show. Walking into the charming house, I allowed them to take my coat and bring me a cocktail to help ease the nervousness we all felt.

I had taken special pains when dressing for this scenario and tried to look somewhat sexy. Another plus to this journey is that I was getting better at noticing what fit my body better and showed off my assets in a more appealing way. That evening I had chosen tight black jeans paired with a black lacy camisole that was cut fairly low, showing more cleavage than normal. Simple yet seductive. When her husband commented that I looked beautiful, silently I appreciated the extra time spent.

I took a seat on the couch, with Wifey sitting next to me and her husband in a chair across from me. They were a very good-looking couple, and again looked and appeared very normal. After a small and slightly awkward get-to-know-you banter, we switched gears and started brainstorming about the best way to get this party started. The couple suggested they could go to their bedroom and start with foreplay, while I used the restroom and made myself more comfortable. Once I was ready, I should join them in the bedroom. Approving the plan, I went to the bathroom and checked myself in the mirror. My nerves were starting up again, and I was immediately filled with questions. Should I take my clothes off and walk into the room naked? Should I give them five minutes? Ten minutes? What was normal in this situation? Taking a deep breath, I smiled back at myself, almost chuckling out loud at my indecisiveness. Jump in with both feet, I reminded myself. Stripping down to my red lace bra and matching panties, I ventured into their bedroom at the end of the hall. The couple wasn't even immediately aware when I walked into the bedroom; they were in their own sexy world. Both naked, sprawled out on their enormous bed, they were locked in a passionate embrace. Quietly taking in the erotic scene, my nervousness faded and sexual desire took over.

As if hearing my thoughts, they looked up from their embrace and eagerly extended their arms so I could join them. As I wiggled in between their warm bodies, Wifey immediately took the lead and wrapped her arms around me, passionately kissing me, loving that her husband was watching us. As we kissed, I felt the softness of her mouth and lips, slightly teasing my tongue with hers. My naked body was on top of hers, and I couldn't help but run my hands down the curves of her body. She felt amazing. Husband, who was already done with watching, pulled me away from her and next to him on the bed. Once he had me close, he inched down, his mouth now between my legs. Just feeling his warm breath so close to me drove me wild. My hands found their way to the back of his head where I gently pushed him into me, unable to withstand the suspense any longer. Hungrily he began licking and sucking, driving me wild. As he licked, Wifey let her own tongue explore my body, landing on my tits. Gently she sucked and tugged at my nipples, loving the way it made me moan with delight. With both of their tongues pleasuring me, I felt my body starting to lose control. Cumming hard, as moans got louder, they licked and sucked harder, helping me enjoy the climax. As I tried to collect myself, Wifey made it clear that she was next. Moving up my body, she brought her own pussy to my lips, straddling my face. It was the first time I had tasted a woman, and the scent, the feeling, and the taste fueled me to grab her hips and pull her body down deeper onto my face. As she moaned and bucked her hips wildly, I knew she was orgasming, and I wanted to taste her every drop.

Husband then lay down on the bed, and Wifey whispered to me that it was his fantasy to have two women suck him off at the same time. Who was I to say no to fulfilling a fantasy? Diving in, I took his entire cock in my mouth, sucking it nice and slow. Wifey positioned herself somewhat under him, and I watched her take his balls in her mouth as I continued to suck. The moment was so sexy, and soon he began to moan uncontrollably. I motioned to her, asking if she wanted to catch his load in her mouth, and she waved me on. His huge load exploded in my mouth, some dribbling down my chin.

Wifey then whispered, "I want to fuck you." I emphatically nodded, and then watched as she pulled out a strap-on from her nightstand. I was so curious and excited as I watched her step into the contraption, securing it on her tiny waist, and running her hand along the giant faux cock. Gently pushing me onto the bed and onto all fours, she took her place behind me and pushed inside me. Husband took his place between her legs, licking on his wife, and she was inside me. This feeling, while familiar, was erotically new, knowing that a woman was fucking me. Glancing over my shoulder, I watched her thrust her cock deep inside me, her hands grasping my hips. Her eyes were closed, and she was softly moaning.

As Wifey finished with me, her husband switched positions with her, keeping me on all fours, but he was now behind me. Wifey was next to him, and I soon felt her fingers guiding his hard cock into my ass. I squealed as he pushed inside that tight space, feeling a small amount of pain and an intense amount of pleasure. I heard the approval from Wifey as she watched his cock deep inside my ass, his balls slapping against my butt with each thrust. He continued pumping until he came again.

We lay in a heap on the bed, sweating and breathing heavily. Our legs and arms entwined in each other's, no one wanting the evening to end. But in the end, it had to, and I needed to head home. As I started to dress, the couple, still on the bed, couldn't stop raving about the encounter. They were already hoping that I would consider joining them again, or even consider being a "regular" friend a couple times a month. I smiled, letting them know that I had a great time as well and would be in touch.

We chatted a few more times in the future, but I never hooked up with them again, much to their disappointment. Again, I felt it would be so hard to recreate these special, magical moments. Not to mention, the excitement for me was really in the surprise of the unknown.

Chapter 17

"My car is making a funny pinging sound on the highway," I told a coworker one day at work. "Take it to the mechanics just down the street. They are great and won't rip you off," he advised. Nodding, I took the number he had written down on scratch paper and went to make the call. Luckily, the gentleman I spoke with said to bring it in that afternoon.

Pulling up to the small garage, I looked around skeptically, silently hoping they were better with cars than they were at making their shop look presentable. The doorbell chimed as I walked through the door, and I quickly scanned the room while I was waiting for someone to realize I was there. It was a poor excuse for a lobby or waiting area. There were two rickety-looking chairs, looking as though they might collapse under a significant amount of weight. A water cooler was in the corner, but no water and no cups. Shrugging, I tapped my fingers on the counter, still waiting to be helped. Maybe I had gone to the wrong mechanic shop. I pulled the paper from my pocket, double-checking the address. Nope, this was it. Impatiently, I sighed, almost irritated with my wasted time there.

Just as I was about to walk out and try another shop, the door to the shop opened, and in walked the mechanic. He flashed me an apologetic smile. "I hope you haven't been waiting here too long. It's been a busy day, and I am the only one here." Immediately whatever irritation I had felt was gone. "I just got here," I lied, flashing him a smile back. Filling him in on the pinging sound my car was making, he said he was happy to take a look. He reached out for my keys, taking them from my hand. I swear I felt his hands linger for just a moment longer than they needed to, but I dismissed the thought, thinking I was just crazy. I looked at him, meeting his gaze for a split second, and felt my stomach flip flop.

Taking a seat in the dingy waiting room, I grabbed the only magazine that was on the counter in front of me. *Popular Mechanics* it read on the cover, and I quickly rolled my eyes and replaced it back to where I had grabbed it. No, thanks. Standing up, I looked through the window into the garage. The mechanic had the hood up on my car and was working intently under the hood. Taking a closer look at him, I tried to understand why my stomach had done a flip-flop during our quick meeting. Looking beyond the smear of oil on his cheek (which was sexy), I saw a bronzed handsome face with a mess of tousled blond hair. His dirty work shirt had his name embroidered on the pocket and clung to his body, allowing me to notice his toned physique. Surprisingly, his hands were what I was most intrigued with—big strong hands, covered in dirt and grime, but oh, so manly. "Ma'am?" His voice startled me back to reality. "Do you want to follow me out to your car and I can explain the problem?" Nodding, I followed him to the garage.

Leaning under the hood together, he started explaining what the problem was. He was standing so close to me, I had trouble focusing on what he was saying. I just kept watching his strong hands, thinking of them on my body. Sensing that my mind was elsewhere, and I that I wasn't paying attention, he switched gears, and his voice became more playful and challenging.

"Penny for your thoughts?"

Blushing, I replied. "My apologies for not paying attention. My mind was on something else. Please continue." Then I did my best to stand up straighter and try to look interested in what he had been saying.

"Well, can I hear where or what your mind was on? From the look on your face, I am curious to know."

Surprised by his persistence, I decided to confess. "You're very sexy and handsome, and I was just admiring your big strong hands." Almost dying inside, I held my breath to see his reaction. I even shocked myself on how brazen I had been. Time on the website was teaching me to be more comfortable in speaking my mind.

"These dirty hands?" He held them up for me to see. I swear he emphasized the word *dirty*.

"Yes, those hands," I whispered.

"What were you thinking about these hands?"

"I was picturing them on my body."

I think you could have heard a pin drop at that moment. Our eyes were locked on each other, the sexual tension thick in the air.

Breaking my gaze, he took my hand and led me back into the lobby. Going through a small door, reading *Employees Only*, we entered a small office. Noticing a desk in the middle of the office, he patted the top of it, suggesting I sit down. My heart was practically beating out my chest waiting to see what happened next. I sat on the edge of the desk, my legs hanging down the side of it. Approaching me, he positioned his body, standing between my legs, facing me. Grabbing my chin in his hand, he turned my face upward to look at him. "I want my hands all over your body." Feeling wet with anticipation, I eagerly nodded. "But I am going to take my time with you." Leaning in, he gently took my bottom lip between his teeth, pulling and biting just enough to make my knees weak. It was a good thing I was sitting down, as I don't think I would have been able to stand.

Standing up straight again, his hands found their way to my blouse buttons. Slowly he undid them one by one until my shirt fell open. I was silently thinking I was so glad that I had decided to wear my black lacy bra instead of my grandma beige one that day. Pulling the straps off my shoulder, he pulled my bra down to my waist, exposing my tits. Staring hungrily at them, he glanced up at me and smiled. His motions, so very slow and methodical, I don't think I had ever experienced someone so good at building anticipation. "How did you picture my hands on your body?"

"I wanted to feel them holding my tits."

Just as I had imagined, his strong hands made their way to my chest, tugging at my nipples until I was groaning with delight. Loving the sounds I made, he pulled at them harder, making me squirm with pleasure. Taking my tits into his mouth, I felt the sharp pain of his teeth closing on them. Whimpering, I begged him to do it harder. The pain, although intense, was exhilarating. Stepping back, he fumbled with his belt and blue jeans, allowing them to slide down around his ankles. I stared at the bulge in front of me, masked behind his underwear. I reached out to assist him with the last layer, but he pushed me back onto the desk, shaking his head.

Obeying his silent command, I sat and watched. He slid his underwear down, and my eyes didn't stray from the cock in front of me. Completely at full attention, it was at least ten inches long. I ached to know what it would feel like inside me. Grabbing his cock in his hands, he again met my gaze. "Penny for your thoughts?" he asked again, smiling, a look of entertainment sparkled in his eyes.

"I want to feel that cock inside me."

"Patience, baby. All in good time."

Coming back closer to me, he slowly pushed my skirt up my thighs. Kneeling on the ground in front of me, grabbing my panties, he slowly pulled them down and tossed them to the side. Pushing my legs apart with his hands, I felt his warm breath on my pussy. He hadn't even touched me yet, but I could feel myself trembling.

Finally feeling his tongue slowly lick me, I cried out in pleasure. With my feet resting on his shoulders, he continued to eat me and I lay back on his desk. He felt so good. Coming up to kiss me, his lips and cheeks were still wet from my juices. As we kissed, my hands found their way to his cock, and sliding up and down around it, I whispered that I wanted him inside me. Climbing onto the desk so that he was on top of me, he held his cock at my opening, rubbing it on me, teasing me. He was relentless.

Finally sliding into me, he went to work. Grabbing my legs, he put them on his shoulders, allowing me to feel him deep inside of me. I looked up at him, watching him do me, and it drove me wild. "Bend me over this desk," I whispered. Climbing off of me, he helped me up, and then pushed me so I was completely bent over the desk. Waiting to feel his cock, I was pleasantly surprised to feel his tongue back inside me. As it flicked in and out of me, I moaned again, hoping this moment would never end.

His hands now back around me, grabbing my tits, I felt his cock plunge back into me. As he fucked me, he told me how good I tasted and how good his cock felt inside me. His words made me hornier, and we pumped harder and faster until we were both cumming at the same time. Both breathing heavy, we stood up and started to get dressed. Picking up my panties, I laughed at how wet they still were. "Nicely done," I said, complimenting him.

Walking back out to my car, he didn't even try to go through the spiel this time. "It's fixed." He laughed. As he opened my door for me, I slid into the driver's seat. Again, cupping my chin in his hand, he leaned over and kissed me. "Come in for service anytime."

"Will do." I smiled. I started my car and drove away.

Chapter 18

My season of adventure reminded me of an episode of *Eat Pray Love*, only maybe the X-rated version. There was so much to see and do in this new world of mine. Thinking back to the time I had enjoyed with the couple I had met online, I logged in one evening, thinking that I may give another one a try. It wasn't something that would be a lifelong fetish, but, again, I had a good time, and the element of surprise is always a teasing and enticing thing. The site was already set up to still search for couples, so I had already received several new emails asking if I wanted to play. One email immediately caught my eye, a very good-looking couple looking for a single female. The ad was written by the female (which was always rare), and she mentioned in her ad that it was her boyfriend's birthday and she was looking at getting him a very special gift. She didn't want to participate, but she wanted to perhaps watch and let him have a good time. Sounded interesting. I responded to her, letting her know that I was up to the task and to let me know details.

Now, still being naive in this sexual world, most of these interactions sounded like fun, and as I had mentioned in my profile I was ready to try most things once, maybe twice.

Knowing what I know now, I would never again venture into a situation where I was a single female, meeting up with a couple that had never done this before. I know that a lot of things may sound sexier and enticing when you read about it or talk dirty with someone about it, but as the interaction becomes real, I think it is difficult for a couple to process what is truly happening and to control their emotions. Especially as a female, with female emotions, if I was truly in love with someone, I think I would have a really hard time watching my significant other be with another woman. Strict rules need to be put into play, and only go as far as they are comfortable.

Hindsight is 20/20, and I went into this situation as I had approached all of my other sexual adventures, ready to make the most of it and enjoy myself to the fullest extent. The girlfriend and I had made plans that I would meet them at a bar, and after a few cocktails come sit with them, flirt with her boyfriend, and she would reveal to him that I was his present for the evening. How could anything go wrong? Promptly at ten p.m. I arrived at the bar. I saw them doing shots at the bar, and as she and I made eye contact, I gave her a quick nod and sat down in the stool next to her boyfriend. He looked over at me, and I introduced myself. "Nice to meet you," he said, then turned back toward his cocktail. I then leaned in a bit closer to him and whispered in his ear that I thought he was extremely handsome and sexy. I definitely wasn't lying when I told him that. He was a big guy, tall, about six feet, broad shoulders, and built tough. His T-shirt clung to his formed biceps, and I felt a sudden desire to reach out and touch them. I refrained from doing so. He blushed at my comment, loving it but surprised at the forwardness of my introduction. I even surprised myself a bit with my confidence. I had come a long way since the unhappy, divorced woman who knew that there was so much more in life and more fun to be had.

Just as he was about to respond to my introduction, his girlfriend appeared at his side and smiled at the both of us. He looked confused at first, assuming that she would be mad at the fact he was speaking to another girl, but in fact she looked the opposite. "Why don't you buy her a drink?" she told him. Looking confused and bewildered, I had to giggle at his look of shock. She then told him, "Happy birthday, babe. She's all yours for the night." The look he wore was priceless. He nodded, understanding the full scope of the situation, and then turned back to me, asking what I would like to drink.

His girlfriend was a social butterfly, working the room, chatting with people, leaving us alone and lost in our own little world. His hand comfortably rested on my thigh, and he was feeling pretty excited about his new birthday present. He whispered all the things he wanted to do with me. Smiling and egging on the situation, I told him it was taking all the self-control I had not to climb into his lap and have him run those big strong hands across my body. With that comment, he excused himself to go speak with his girlfriend. Watching their interaction, it looked more serious than I would have imagined. She looked at me as he continued to talk, nodded, and then walked over. Putting her hand on my shoulder, she explained that her boyfriend wasn't feeling the vibe from me. He was no longer interested in getting together with me and her that evening, and he wanted to go home.

I was shocked. Literally the sexual tension could have been cut with a knife, or so I had thought. Feeling silly and a little embarrassed, I nodded back at her, said no problem, shrugging it off like my ego wasn't bruised. Feeling still confused, I couldn't believe that I had mixed up the signals that badly. I swore he had been having a good time as well. I looked up as I saw them leaving the bar, and saw boyfriend turn back, looking directly at me, winking. Did I just see that? I thought. What does that mean? Dismissing the wink, I ordered another cocktail.

About twenty minutes later, I was paying my tab to leave, when my phone lit up with an unrecognized number. I hesitantly answered and heard the deep voice on the other end of the phone say hello. I realized it was her boyfriend, as we had traded numbers while talking at the bar. Before I had a chance to say anything, he was apologizing to me for the situation that had just unfolded. What he told me next shocked me. "I want you so badly, but I want you all to myself. I don't want my girlfriend around. I want to fuck you like you deserved to be fucked, just me and you. So I made up a lie that I was not attracted to you, wanted to leave, and then I took my girlfriend home. I am at my house now, and I would love it if you would come over and let me have my way with you."

This is not your typical situation that happens in romance books. Did I just get asked to be side action? Was I going to be the other woman? While trying to decide what to do, I was well aware of the little voice inside my head telling me not to go. Now, while I would love to say that I didn't go to his house that evening, I cannot. All of the cocktails that I had consumed throughout the evening, partnered with the echoing sound of what he wanted to do to me sexually, took over. I texted him to send me the address.

After pulling up to his house, I didn't even have to knock before the door swung open and he was ushering me into the foyer. Grabbing me in his arms, he plunged his tongue deep into my mouth, kissing me with reckless abandonment. During our conversation at the bar, he had mentioned a fantasy that he had. He had always wanted a woman to wear his Seahawks jersey, with no panties on, bending over, ready to be nasty. As he pulled me into his living room, I saw a jersey folded up on the floor in front of the fireplace. Pushing him onto the sofa, I picked up the jersey and headed into the restroom. Coming out, he was like an eager little puppy staring from the couch, excited for what was to come next. Dressed in his jersey and nothing else, I climbed up on the opposite end of the couch and leaned over the end, allowing him to have a full view of me. Before I could even blink, he was behind me, and I could feel his cock pressed up against me begging to be let out of his pants.

Pulling his pants off, while keeping me bent over the couch, he entered me, aggressively, while his hands grabbed my shoulders pulling me down hard and fast onto his cock. The deepness he was able to get gave me goose bumps down to my toes. He flipped me over, still draped across the couch, still inside me, while his hands went to work on my tits and his tongue flitted in and out of my mouth. The jersey by then had hit the floor, and our naked, sweaty bodies worked hard into the night. About two hours later, I found myself calling "uncle," as I was exhausted. Lying back on the couch, he proceeded to lick every inch of my body, arousing it enough to go for round two.

Late into the night, exhausted, I got up and started to get dressed. He appeared behind me, cupping my breasts in his hands, wanting me to stay the night. Telling him I couldn't, I continued getting dressed, while his hands continued to grope and explore my body. I would put something on, and he would take it off again. He brought his mouth to my tits, slightly nibbling on my nipples, one then the other. Hearing me start to moan, he continued more aggressively, biting sharply on my nipple. My knees nearly gave way from the pleasure I felt. As he continued to bite one nipple, he pinched the other nipple between his fingers, sensing my delight in what he was doing. Laughing, I gave up and climbed on his lap for round three. His big strong arms held me tight so I wouldn't get away.

We both woke in the morning, feeling the sunshine through the windows on our faces. We had fallen asleep on the couch, the couch where we had sex on every inch of it and in every position. I could feel my body tingle as I recalled the fun from last night. He reached over, kissed me on the cheek while his hands wandered south, and found their way inside me. Moaning, I could feel my hips start to automatically move with the thrusts of his fingers. He felt so good. He slid on top of me, and inside me, once more thrusting his cock in a rhythmic motion. We grinded on each other until I felt him cumming and moaning with pleasure. "Stay the weekend with me. Don't leave," he pleaded.

Watching him get up and walk to the shower, I knew I had to leave. Quickly throwing on my clothes, I gulped a quick cup of coffee that he had made for me and sneaked out the door.

Pulling up at my house, I heard my phone ping. I looked down, realizing it was his girlfriend. Guilt hit me like a ton of bricks. I opened her message, freezing in my tracks when I read it. She knew I had spent the night with her boyfriend. Getting a strange vibe from him last night, she had driven past his house later in the evening once he had dropped her off. That's when she saw my car and put the story together. Within her text, she proceeded to call me all the names that I knew I deserved, as well as threatening me for lying to her and for having sex with her partner. I sent her a reply, apologizing profusely for what I had done, but knowing that would not be enough. I vowed I would not see her boyfriend again, and I needed to just leave this situation alone. Drama and wrecking homes were definitely not what I had signed up for when I started this adventure. Now her boyfriend was texting me, telling me what I had already known, that we had been discovered she was furious with him.

He said he didn't care, that he had been done with her anyway, and he wanted to see me again.

In that moment, all I could feel was sympathy for his girlfriend. Before all this had transpired, while she and I had been planning and texting, she confessed her true love for her boyfriend. They had been together for two years and she had been hoping for a ring at the upcoming holidays. He had always talked about having a threesome with her and had been pressuring her to invite someone else into the bedroom to satisfy his craving. Hence the reason she had reached out to me to make him happy and help fulfill his fantasy.

I never responded to her boyfriend, blocking his number on my phone to avoid any temptation. While the sex had been amazing, I could never forgive myself if I had continued with the situation. I discovered that in sexual exploration, no matter what curiosity or fetish you have, if your partner is not completely on board, then it is up to you to find a different partner or to relinquish the idea of the fetish. If you decide to find a different partner, one that might make you happier and is into more sexual adventures that match yours, let the other down in the most appropriate and respectful way. I was learning that each person had a different level of comfort of need in this sexual world, and everyone's level should be accepted.

Chapter 19

It was safe to say that I could officially check the box involving couples off my list. I had dabbled, had a good time, but as the last adventure ended with a bad taste in my mouth, I decided to go back to single men hookups. Fewer people, less drama, is how I figured. I wasn't in this to break up relationships, or to become a friend with benefits. I really wanted just the benefits; I really wasn't even wanting the friend part of it. And knowing myself, the longer I spent with someone, the more I knew feelings would develop, and that wasn't an option for me at the point in my exploration. There were still differences between men and women, I felt, about how we attached. Having sex would be easy, but spending time with someone was a bit more challenging.

Coming home late one night from a grueling day at work, I threw my laptop on the table and collapsed on my living room chair. I had dealt with several daunting employee issues that day, as well as a deadline from my boss, and not to mention a bitchy customer. Over it, I poured myself a drink, enjoying the quiet. Taking a sip of the handmade cocktail, I thought, you know what would be better than this cocktail, great sex. Sex without any type of commitment, with someone who didn't even care about knowing my name. Just help me eliminate some of this built-up tension and then leave me alone. I chuckled, remembering a quote from Charlie Sheen that the reason he paid hookers was not to have sex with him, but to leave after the fact. I totally understood what he had meant by it. Sometimes, you don't want to have any strings.

Opening my computer, I was intent to find the perfect low-key hookup, maybe even for that evening. Scanning through the usual invites and come-ons, I quickly selected a nice-looking man who had sent me a note asking for a meet-up for some discreet fun. I noticed he was currently online, so I messaged him to see what his plans were for the evening.

He immediately texted me back, giving me his phone number. I responded with a text, "Let's go fuck. Tell me when and where, and I'll meet you there." It took mere minutes to get a response, and I thought that he was probably thinking there is no way this person is real. He responded with a location, asking to meet him in the parking lot, in his large SUV. Game on. The meeting time was in an hour, and truly I didn't even feel the need to prep and gussy myself up for this meeting. In my mind, this meeting was raw and purposeful, and then I never wanted to see this person again.

I threw on jeans and a sweater, a ball cap and tennis shoes, and headed to the meeting spot. It was dark, and I had hoped that he had a strong tint on his windows. Pulling into the parking lot, sitting at the far end was a tan Cadillac Escalade. I pulled up along the side and got out of the car. The trunk to the Cadillac opened, and my good-looking stranger flashed me a big smile from inside.

"Still down for this?" he asked. I hopped in and closed the trunk behind me.

Hot writhing lust was how I describe this encounter. There was no need for foreplay or passionate kissing. He was sliding my soaked panties off moments after I hopped into his rig. Bringing his mouth between my legs, his tongue did not disappoint. He licked every inch of me, making me moan with pleasure. I traded the favor, pulling his pants down and taking his cock deep in my mouth. It was at that moment I noticed his cock was pierced. This was a first for me, and I looked up at him. "Trust me, you'll like it," he whispered. I continued for several minutes licking and sucking until I couldn't stand it any longer. I needed to feel him in me.

I turned away from him and got on all fours. Grabbing my hips, he plunged into me, making me gasp. Grabbing a fistful of my hair, he continued to pump his cock deep inside me. The slight pain from the hair pulling made the situation that much hotter, and I started telling him to fuck me harder. He pumped harder and faster, and then I felt his big hand smack my ass. I loved it. He noticed I was thoroughly enjoying myself and continued with the spankings.

He had been right about the piercing. It hit me in all the right spots and had me cumming faster and harder than I would normally. I made a mental note during sex that if I were to find another guy that had a piercing, I would see if I had the same results.

Finishing up, he kissed me, and then opened the door for me. I hopped out, said goodbye, and got into my car. I couldn't believe how simple that was. I wasn't sad to leave him, or didn't feel that I was missing out on anything. I got what I wanted, and he got his. Driving home, I turned on the radio and sang along to music. Amazing what good sex can do for a bad mood.

Chapter 20

Dropping my daughter off at her dad's, I sighed from exhaustion. Work had been grueling that week, paired with school and riding lessons for the kid, I was ready to forget about commitments for the weekend and take a little me time. Looking at myself in the mirror earlier that week I noticed my gray roots starting to peek through my normal blond highlights, and my eyebrows were in desperate need of a wax. Who was I kidding, my whole body was in need of a wax.

Hitting pause on my hectic schedule seemed like a dream as I booked several appointments for my self-care. Hair appointment at ten, facial and waxing at one, and then complete the day with a massage.

Feeling like a million bucks, I let my robe hit the floor as I climbed onto the massage bed and snuggled underneath the warm comforter. Against my freshly waxed skin, the blanket felt smooth and luxurious. Closing my eyes, I waited for my masseuse.

I heard a slight, soft voice saying hello as she entered the massage room. Telling her hello back, I tried to think how long it had been since I had treated myself to a massage. Too long, I thought. Starting at my shoulders and back, she asked how the pressure was. "It's great," I answered.

She used long soft strokes down my back, moving down toward my butt. Her touch, soft yet firm, felt wonderful. I closed my eyes, enjoying the moment. She continued to my butt cheeks, squeezing one than the other. A bit surprised that she was massaging my butt cheeks, as that normally wasn't allowed, my senses shifted, from relaxed to feeling slightly aroused. Asking again if everything felt okay, I felt myself nod. "Mmmm-hmmm."

As she adjusted to the lower part of my butt, I felt the comforter slip down to my lower legs. Knowing my ass was exposed to her, my sexual desire went into overdrive. I was extremely turned on that she was looking at me, touching my body, and I wanted to feel more of her hands. I felt my body naturally start to slowly move in unison with her strokes, eager to feel her next touch. I knew she sensed my excitement, knowing I was getting turned on by her touch.

Though her hands were still mainly on my butt, she flirted with my pussy, framing the outside of it with her fingers with each stroke. My body was almost trembling from the excitement. "Turn over," she said gently. Flipping over, I put my head on the pillow and waited to feel the blanket over my body. The blanket never found its way back to my body.

Her gentle hands gently found their way back to me, starting at my shoulders. Keeping my eyes closed, I eagerly wondered what would happen next. Her hands slid down from my shoulders, cupping and rubbing my tits. I inhaled deeply, feeling the sensation, loving every moment. As she pinched my nipples, first softly and then with more force, a groan escaped from my lips. I couldn't help myself, it felt so good. Slightly opening my eyes, I saw her intently looking at my tits as she fondled them. She caught my glance and smiled at me. She then took her index finger to her lips. "Shhhh." Nodding, I closed my eyes again.

I felt her warm breath on my nipples, and then I felt her lips close on them. She suckled and nibbled, sharing each one equally, spending quality time. My hips continued to move, bucking ever so slightly, aching for her to touch me more. Sensing this, I felt her slide down the table, gently pushing my legs apart. Her fingers began to explore me, opening my entrance, gently sliding in and out. Quietly moaning, I begged her for more. Feeling her tongue enter me, I rocked my body in time to her licks. Taking her time with me, she slowly licked me from front to back. Over and over again she continued this motion until I felt myself cumming. Trying to stay quiet, I gripped the sides of the table to keep from screaming in pleasure.

I opened my eyes, exhausted from pleasure to see her looking at me.

"You like?" she asked.

"Oh, yes." I nodded. "Very much."

Looking satisfied, she pulled out warm towels from the nearby closet and proceeded to slowly wipe the oil from my body.

"Me too." She giggled. With that, she found her way out of the room.

Chapter 21

Driving back to visit my small hometown, about two hours west of Seattle, for a birthday party for one of my dearest friends, I was looking forward to catching up with the gang. It had been a little while since I had seen everyone, and my girlfriends had made it clear that they were worried about me. Since the divorce, I had thrown myself into work (or so they thought), not taking as much time as I used to, to catch up with random girls' nights. My group of friends are so special to me. Most of them date back to junior high and high school years. Together we shared crazy college memories as roommates and continued those friendships as we got married and started families. The thing I loved most is no matter how much time had passed, we always were there for each other, and always able to pick up exactly where we had left off, months or even years later.

While I was excited to see them all, I also felt a little pang of loneliness.

I longed to be able to tell my closest friends about the other activity I was throwing myself into since the divorce. I had yet to tell anyone about my adventures on the adult website. When I thought about telling them, I pictured their disappointed faces looking at me with shame and embarrassment *We thought you had more class than this,* or *Wow, you have a daughter, and you should be acting like a mom, not a nineteen-year-old teenybopper.* Those were the words I would imagine they would say to me. I couldn't bear the thought of having to explain myself, especially because I still felt that I was classy. And I *know* I am a good mother, but the thought of perhaps someone questioning that was something I don't think I could stand. I would do absolutely anything for my daughter. The question in my head still lingered, even with a child, and even with being a successful career woman, why can't a woman choose to explore her sexual desires and still be a role model? One of the many double standards that women had to deal with. I shook my head. "Mum's the word," I said aloud in the car. They couldn't find out.

Pulling up to my girlfriend's house, I was instantly greeted with hugs and kisses from my people. I basked in the comfort of friendship and laughed as the group started to bombard me with questions about my life. Holding up the time-out hand gesture, I excused myself to get a drink and wish my friend's husband a happy birthday. He smiled warmly at me, embracing me into a bear hug and whispered, "Don't let them get to you, they are just worried about you. We all love you." Tears sprang to my eyes for a mere moment at the kindness that I hadn't realized I was missing. He saw that I was starting to get a little emotional, so he threw me a beer, smacked me on the ass, and yelled, "Now get out of here and have fun."

Grinning, I cracked open the beer and wandered through the charming, familiar farmhouse. The walls were filled with pictures of their happy family. Aside from a loving marriage, they had two boys that were great kids. I had watched them grow up, remembering moments of holding them when they were just babies. I found myself growing envious as I continued down the hallway, wishing for a fleeting moment that I had what they had. A long marriage filled with love and laughter through the years and two beautiful boys that were the highlight of their lives. A small part of me yearned for the love and stability that they had found in each other.

Shaking off the feeling of envy, and embracing the love that I felt for them, I went back to my awaiting friends. We drank, gossiped about people, ate too much, and laughed until our bellies hurt. Around two in the morning, the party finally started to break up, and most people were heading home. Planning on crashing on their couch for the night, I changed into my jammies and curled up on the couch. As people headed out the door, one of my dear friends from high school came over and apologized that we hadn't even had a moment that evening to catch up. I patted the empty cushion next to me, and asked him, "Well, why not now?"

He smiled and sank into the sofa. It was good to see him; it had been a while. I had known him since junior high, and he was the first boy I had ever kissed. Although, I think he was the first kiss for a lot of girls back then! He had aged well, and we had all hung out in the same circle since school. So it was never a surprise to catch him at one of these friend get-togethers. We had never dated outside of seventh grade; he was just always a good friend.

"Good night," my girlfriend and her husband told me as they turned off the lights and headed to bed. My girlfriend gave me a wink and a small smile before flipping the switch. I think she was hoping that something was going to happen and sparks would fly with our friend.

High School Guy and I proceeded to catch up on all our mutual friends and what had been going on with life in general. He expressed his apologies regarding my divorce and asked how things had been since then. "A little lonely," I lied, even though I had been having a great time. Although this evening I had been feeling a little sorry for myself, and I thought why stop now. With that last comment he leaned into me and softly kissed my lips. Whether this was a good idea or whether it was fulfilling another need that I currently had, I pulled him closer, kissing him more passionately. He responded eagerly.

We didn't make love that evening, as we were not in love, but we did not fuck either. It was softer and more tender than just getting laid. He took his time with me, held me in his arms;

each move was slow and filled with passion. It was just what I needed, and I felt that because he knew me, he might have known what I had needed as well. Once we finished, he kissed me goodbye and headed home.

My tongue felt fuzzy, and my head was pounding as I awoke to my girlfriend's dog climbing on me, licking my face, excited to have a stranger on his couch. I didn't hear anyone else in the house stirring yet, so I assumed everyone was still sleeping. I found my way into the kitchen, searching through the cabinets until I located a bottle of aspirin. Just as I had swallowed three of them, I heard the excited voice of my girlfriend.

"Well?" she questioned. I nodded, and she let out a squeal of delight.

"Shhhh. Everyone is still sleeping," I scolded. She shook her head and motioned that everyone was already up. The boys had already gone to practice, and her husband had left to go get us coffee. Sensing we were talking about him, her husband walked in with hot Starbucks in hand. As I happily accepted the coffee, thanking him with a kiss on the cheek, my girlfriend was already dragging me back to the couch to hear all the details.

Driving back home, my thoughts turned to last night. The small details were still a bit fuzzy due to the many drinks I had consumed over the evening, but I understood I had been a bit sad, and my friend had comforted me in a way that made me feel not so lonely. As if reading my mind, I heard my phone beep with an incoming text. It was High School Guy telling me that he had an amazing time last night and he wanted to see me again. Soon. I finished my drive home, not sure what to tell him. There was a small attraction to him, and he was a good friend. I just wasn't sure if this was something worth continuing.

Not wanting to tell him no and that I didn't want to see him, I accepted an invitation to go to a movie with him the following night. Maybe it was something I needed to give a chance and see if there were real feelings that could develop into more. He picked me up at my house, which given the last few months felt strange that a guy could know where I lived. I hopped in the passenger seat, gave him a hug, and we headed off.

Arriving at the theater, he grabbed my hand as we walked in. Things felt natural, and I enjoyed the company, glad that I had decided to go out with him. After the movie, he asked if I wanted to go to his place, and I nodded. His roommates were there playing beer pong with some friends. We laughed and drank more than our fair share. It was a great time. After a couple hours of beer pong, I found myself yawning. High School Guy caught me and smiled. Motioning to his bedroom, he told everyone we were heading to bed.

I couldn't believe how tired I was, but I was not a young one anymore, and this staying out late and drinking was something I hadn't done in a long time. Sowing your wild oats was hard work.

We started to undress, and High School Guy led me over to his bed. Sitting down on the edge I undid my pants and wiggled out of them, then slid my panties down until they gently fell in a heap on the floor. He gently pushed me back on to the bed so my legs were still hanging down and my body was completely on the bed. He then kneeled on the floor, and I felt his warm breath between my legs. As his hands ran up and down my thighs and his tongue continued to work on me, I thought how I wished I felt that burning sexual desire in this moment. But I didn't. I felt no attraction and no spark.

"Are you sleeping?" He sounded shocked. I quickly woke, realizing in horror that I had fallen asleep as he was trying to pleasure me. "No," I lied, but he already had his feelings hurt. Apparently, I had started snoring. I felt horrible and tried to apologize as he climbed into bed. He tried to just brush it off, turning over in bed so he was not facing me.

"Let's just go to sleep," he muttered. We went to sleep, and in the morning it was just as awkward. I was up early, and again apologized for my behavior (or lack thereof) from last night. I got dressed and gave him a quick kiss on the cheek. I had already subconsciously known that he was not the guy for me but had hoped that things would have worked out better than this.

Chapter 22

Grabbing my bag on the luggage carousel I headed outside to hail a cab to my hotel. I was in San Francisco for the week for work, and I wanted to get checked in, relax, and watch the Seahawks play in the *Monday Night Football* game. It was a quick ten-minute ride to the hotel. I paid for the cab and headed to my room. Collapsing on the bed, I grabbed the remote and went to turn on the TV. Thinking the game might be on at the hotel bar and a cocktail would hit the spot, I threw the remote back on the bed and headed downstairs.

Upon arriving at the bar, I was surprised at how busy it was as I searched for an open stool. There were none, so I leaned in next to a guy at the bar, excused myself, and proceeded to order a drink from the bartender. The guy I leaned over laughed and commented on the Seahawks jersey that I was wearing. As I grabbed my drink, he continued to make conversation, chatting about the game and football in general. He was cute, I thought as I took a long drink of my cocktail. He was dressed casually but professionally in jeans and a sport coat and was drinking a beer. His big smile lit up the room when he laughed, and his bald head was incredibly sexy, as my thoughts immediately went to running my hands over it. Silently laughing, I forced my thoughts back to reality. Looking around, this guy also noticed that all barstools were taken, and surprised me by asking if I wanted to go to a nearby bar to finish watching the game. I nodded, and five minutes later we were walking into a local dive bar.

The next few hours were a whirlwind, and time flew by. He and I talked and laughed as if we had known each other forever. We learned about each other's lives and careers. I learned that he traveled often for work, was quite successful at his job, and was from the Boston area. While super intellectual, it was his sense of humor and sarcasm that immediately won me over. Unfortunately, I found out he was a Patriots fan, but knowing that people cannot be perfect, I thought I would overlook this flaw, continuing to get to know him. Mentioning that San Francisco was an area he traveled to often for work, he volunteered up his company and to show me around the town during my week there. Who was I to say no?

Walking me back to the hotel, it was late, and we both had to work the next day. He held my hand on the walk back, and then pleasantly surprised me in the hotel lobby when he pulled me to him and kissed me gently on the lips. "Good night," he whispered, and then disappeared into an elevator to his room. As I got ready for bed, the smile on my face would not fade.

The next morning came quick, and I had to drag myself out of bed for a quick shower. Picking up my phone, I noticed it was lit up showing a text from him. Immediately I felt a smile come to my lips. I had a wonderful time last night, and I was looking forward to seeing him again. He had texted, asking if we could get a quick coffee together before we both had to be at work. Yes! I screamed to myself. I met Boston Guy about forty-five minutes later in the lobby. My heart skipped a beat when I saw him, and he gave me a hug that made me want to drag him off to my room versus even thinking of going to work. We laughed about last night and agreed that we both had had an amazing time. Capitalizing on the moment, he then asked if we could meet up for dinner after work. I nodded, grabbed my coffee, and waved goodbye as I quickly scooted off to work.

All through my lecture my mind was somewhere else, on someone else. He and I texted like school kids that day, back and forth, making jokes and making plans for the evening. The chemistry was unexplainable; it was like I had known this guy my whole life. We agreed to meet at five thirty p.m., have a cocktail, and then see what transpired from there.

When I walked into the bar I could feel myself light up when I saw him. I was drawn to him and was so looking forward to just being around him, hanging out and having fun. He greeted me with the same warmth as the day before, wrapping his arms around me and warmly kissing me on the lips. Also, scoring points as the perfect gentleman, he also had remembered what I had been drinking the night before and already had the drink waiting for me when I arrived. Such an easy but effective move, fellas! Catching up on our day, he then decided to take me to a little place near there known for their delicious tacos and strong margaritas.

The atmosphere between us was electric and almost magical. It was so hard to pinpoint why it was so strong. It was the type of kismet connection that you cannot ever plan, it just must organically happen. I don't think I ever felt his arm leave the small of my back that entire evening, nor did I want it to. Playing pool, chatting with locals, and with our continued in-depth conversations, I felt us growing closer. In the early morning hours of the next day, we stumbled our way back to the hotel and straight to his hotel room. Boston Guy gently lay me down on his bed, climbing in next to me, passionately kissing me. As he slowly undressed me, I helped, shimmying out of my jeans, and then turned my attention to his attire. Pulling off his shirt and pulling him on top of me, I wanted to feel his body against mine. He felt like heaven against my skin. Running his hands through my hair, he continued to kiss me until I couldn't wait any longer. I wanted him so badly. He slid his cock inside me and moaned softly as it entered. I reached around him, grabbing his ass cheeks in my hands and pulling him as deep as I could into me. All night long we had slow, passionate, delicious sex. Between rounds, I would curl up under his arm, and we would sleep for a bit, then wake up, easily and quickly arousing the other for another go-round.

Waking up for work that same morning, I found myself still in bed with him, still tangled up in his arms; neither one of us wanting to get up and leave one another. We cuddled until we literally ran out of time and had to hurry off to work, again in separate directions. The rest of the week continued like this, working during the day, unable to focus on anything else but each other. Thinking about the evening, seeing him, and being with him. The conversations, the kissing, the sex—it was literally something I had never felt before, and I knew that I was starting to develop real feelings for him in this short time.

As the week was coming to an end, he came to see me in my hotel room as I was packing to leave. With both of us feeling a bit sad and vulnerable about such an amazing week coming to an end, we spoke about the future and possibilities. Deep down we both knew that the impossible never works out the way you want it to. We lived on separate coasts, both were extremely busy with work, and we had very separate lives. In a short amount of time, we had grown so close, and now we would have to forget each other and go back to life as we knew it a week ago before we had met.

We sat in each other's arms, holding on to our last few moments together. With my hands on his face, I began to kiss him, feeling my sexual urges quickly spring to life, wanting him one last time. Unbuckling his belt and sliding his jeans down, I then took his hard cock in my mouth. I heard him gasp, then moan with pleasure. I wanted to taste him so badly. Over the course of the week, we had had sex many times, yet I had not had him inside my mouth. The taste and excitement were just as I had imagined. As I sucked his cock, I looked up at him and smiled. The look he gave me back, I will never forget. I continued to lick and suck until I heard his moans get louder and his breathing heavier. He grabbed the back of my head and pushed it deeper onto him as I tasted his cum in my mouth. "Where did that come from?" he questioned breathlessly. I smiled and climbed into the nook of his arm while he closed his eyes and enjoyed the last few moments.

Chapter 23

The year had been one for the books. It had truly been and continued to be all that I had hoped for, and the quest to quench my sexual desire and to experiment out of my comfort zone had been more satisfying than I could have ever imagined. Besides a few hiccups along the way, I had met some amazing people, experienced gratifying interactions, and became more aware of who I was as a person and what I needed to be happy. Now that being said, I was not quite ready to log off entirely from the website, but I was beginning to feel the want and need to be in a relationship again. The adventure was great, but it was time for more.

Logging on one day, I thought I'd browse the offers and scan the pictures for anyone that stood out to me. Normally I wasn't the one to make the first move, but I was feeling the moment, and wanted to see if there was anything I had been missing or hadn't noticed. I stumbled across a profile picture of handsome man with the caption reading Fun Time Guy. The photo was waist up, shirtless, taken in some tropical location. He was wearing sunglasses, so it was hard to get the full scope of his looks, but his smile was great and he was built nicely. He had dark-brown hair, short with a military-type cut, and his golden skin was eye-catching.

I thought I would send out a quick note to say hello and see if he might be interested. Plus, it might be fun for me to make the first move versus wait for the offer to come to me. Once I hit submit, I left for work, and as usual got caught up in the daily grind. A few hours later, taking a quick break, I happened to check my personal email and noticed a new note from Fun Time Guy. I noticed the email was short and lacked punctuation. It just stated that he normally doesn't respond to profiles without photos, but just this time he thought he would write back and see if I was real. I responded that I was indeed real, sending him my prior profile picture to prove it.

Emailing continued back and forth for a day or so before I trusted him enough to share my phone number. Texting was always so much easier to communicate. Fun Time Guy seemed nice enough in our early interactions, and while he wasn't immediately my type personality-wise, there was something that was definitely unique about him. I just couldn't put my finger on it.

Texting was easy with Fun Time Guy. He too was from the Seattle area; however, he spent most of his time working in Alaska. His schedule was cumbersome, as he was in town only every two weeks. Two weeks he spent working on the remote North Slope of Alaska, and then usually the other two were usually spent traveling either to visit family or to catch a tan and get laid in some exotic location. His schedule helped him explain why he was on the website. Coming to town for short stints, it was hard to keep a relationship but easier to just get laid. Understandable. When I asked him about possibility of meeting up at some point, he apologetically shared that his schedule was pretty crazy for the next couple of months and that he wouldn't be coming home for at least two months. Hawaii, back to Alaska, then Houston, back to Alaska, then home, but home with a scheduled surgery for a torn meniscus.

After hearing this schedule, I rolled my eyes, thinking this guy would be a lot of work and time just to get laid. I told him, "Well, we can see what happens, text me when you're in town. Have fun traveling." Thinking nothing more about him and knowing I wasn't going to hold my breath, I went about my day.

Fun Time Guy called me that night. He said even if we can't meet, we can still talk and get to know each other, right?

What could it hurt? I wasn't doing anything anyway. We talked for a couple of hours that evening, sharing stories of our families and childhood, our likes and dislikes, comparing stories about this crazy website. I found he was entertaining and sweet, with an intriguing kinky side that I needed to explore deeper. We talked daily from that point on. I heard about his travels in Hawaii and seeing family in Texas, while he heard about my daily work life and stressors. It was so interesting that without ever meeting someone you could learn so much about them just by long, in-depth conversations.

He was so sweet but completely lacked empathy. A past Army Ranger, Fun Time Guy was extremely passionate about our country and politics. Sports were also his thing, and he could talk for hours about the Seattle Seahawks or Mariners. To him, the best day of the year was the upcoming NFL draft day. An electrician by trade, he was currently running a small crew in the remote area of Prudhoe Bay, Alaska. Rough around the edges, an alpha male to a T, but so damn sexual and so handsome. By sexual standards, he thought a girl who wouldn't give a blow job was a complete deal-breaker. He was forty-five years old, never married, never wanting to get married, and no kiddos. Single as they come and had lived the life to prove that.

Work was busy as ever, and my daughter had quite the budding social calendar as she chose the expensive sport of horse jumping. Things were good, and I was feeling more content these days. Fun Time Guy and I surprisingly were still talking or texting almost daily. Slowly, through our many conversations, we were developing a friendship. At the end of a long and tiring day, I was now even looking forward to hearing his voice at the other end of the phone.

As the timeline grew near to him coming home, he reminded me of his impending knee surgery, still thinking it wasn't the best time to meet up for the first time. His brother would be staying with him to help take care of him, and he wasn't sure how he was even going to feel after the surgery. Together, we agreed to continue to wait, figuring one day it would happen. Why rush it at this point? Plus, my week was booked solid with work and social engagements, so once again, our lives didn't align.

I checked on Fun Time Guy after his surgery to see how he was feeling. I asked if he needed anything, knowing that his answer would most likely be no, but still I wanted to extend the offer. With his brother there, I was sure he had everything he needed. While he thanked me for the gesture, he assured me he was good and in less pain than he had thought he would be. Satisfied he was content, I went about my day, planning that evening to go out with my girlfriends from high school, eager to see them.

Later that day, busy at work, I received a text message from one of my girlfriends that she had sick kiddos and she was unable to meet that night. Disappointed but completely understanding, we all decided at that point to reschedule to a different night. It was quite the drive for all of us to meet up anyway, so better to capture us all together than to have to travel and not get us all there.

As I was packing up my computer to leave work for the day, I shot Fun Time Guy a text letting him know that my plans had changed; I was going to be at home instead of going out, and if he was bored and wanted to chat later, that I would be around. The text that I received back surprised me and caught me off guard. It said, "Well, if you are free and don't mind driving, or the fact that I am on crutches, let's go grab a drink." My heart started to race. After two months of just chatting on the phone, we were finally going to meet. Texting back, I told him that sounded great and that I didn't mind at all. I would pick him up at seven. Glancing quickly in the mirror, I ran my hands through my hair, applied some lipstick, and scooted out the door.

At seven p.m. sharp, I was driving through his condo complex, looking for the house number he had texted to me, my stomach doing flips inside. Since beginning this online journey, this was by far the most nervous I had been for a first date. I couldn't exactly put my finger on why, but I assumed it was because we had been chatting for a while, creating a real friendship versus just a random hookup.

A few feet away I spotted a shadowy figure leaning on crutches near the mailbox hub of the condos. I pulled over and immediately got out of the car to see if he needed help getting in. Standing there, he looked as handsome as ever, dressed in blue jeans and a bright-blue T-shirt. Later, I would find out that a girl he once dated told him that the color blue brings out his blue bedroom eyes. Who says things like that?

Fun Time Guy was leaning on a pair of crutches, a white teddy bear tucked under his arm. Before I could even hug him, he handed me the teddy bear and said it was a polar bear from Alaska for my four-year-old daughter. "I know she doesn't know about me, but you can just tell her a friend got it for her," he said. My heart melted; I literally thought it was one of the sweetest gestures to this day. In a few of our past conversations,

I had mentioned my daughter but was quick to point out that she doesn't meet anyone I date. My role as a mother doesn't overlap with my role as a single woman. I am a mother first and foremost. Understanding and telling me he respected me more for that stance, I was glad to see we were on the same page.

We arrived at a dive bar not too far from his place. It was dead inside, which I was secretly relieved about, and we chose a booth near the pool tables. Over several beers, we found that we chatted as easily as if we were on one of our nightly phone calls. Conversations with him were stimulating to say the least. He was knowledgeable and passionate about so many subjects that I never knew where one conversation would start and how another would finish.

Now face-to-face with Fun Time Guy, I was finally able to get a really good look at him. He really was handsome and physically my type to a T. He was about five eight (although he says five nine) with a stocky build (which I loved). My favorite feature was by far his arm muscles, not even having to flex to spot the biceps. He had a great smile and dark, short hair, and his eyes sparkled when he laughed. His face wore several battle scars that I later found out were from his army days. A bit of a fighter and hothead back in the day, he assured me not to worry, that he had grown up a lot and matured since those days. Silently laughing inside, I took that reasoning with a grain of salt. Men don't mature.

I excused myself to the restroom about an hour into the evening, and when I returned I saw him standing up near the pool tables. Walking over to him, I realized in that moment that we had yet to touch, not even a simple hug hello. I was eager to change that. Meeting him near the tables, I sidled up next to him so that we were almost touching, and told him how glad I was that we had met up. Slowly I inched my face closer to his, hinting at what I wanted. Sensing my want, he met me halfway to the kiss. Electricity shot through me once our lips locked. Kissing him was a feeling of comfort and excitement rolled into one.

Pulling back up at his condo complex, he leaned over in the passenger seat giving me one last soft kiss for the evening. "I'll call you later," he whispered, and disappeared into the darkness.

Chapter 24

"What are you doing this weekend?" my phone lit up the next morning with a text from Fun Time Guy. Smiling, I texted back that I was planning on having a low-key weekend, probably just watching the Apple Cup and the Seahawks game, maybe cleaning the house. Fun Time Guy then suggested that I should watch one of the games with him. His brother had taken the day off from "babysitting" him, and he wanted some company. Agreeing that was a good idea, I decided to head to his place for the Saturday afternoon Apple Cup football game.

Back at his condo, this time knocking on the door, I laughed at my nervousness, realizing how excited I was to see Fun Time Guy. I would have thought seeing him the night before would have satisfied me for a couple of days, but I was so looking forward to just hanging with him and feeling the warmth of his kisses. The door opened, and there he was looking as cute as ever. Dressed in blue jeans and a husky T-shirt, he looked ready for the game. Engulfing me immediately into a hug, I felt as though he was excited to see me too.

Looking around, I couldn't help but take notice of the bachelor pad I had just stepped into. Filled with decor of black and metal furniture, a glass coffee table, and *Playboy* magazines on the back of the toilet, I felt like I had just stepped into a 1980s frat house. Walking into the kitchen, I noticed Fun Time Guy had gotten a plethora of snacks to ensure that the atmosphere felt inviting and like a true football Saturday. Hungrily, we loaded our plates and got comfy on the couch just before kickoff.

Like an excited schoolgirl, I was keenly aware of each time his hand brushed mine or when his leg rested against mine. Halfway through the game, Fun Time Guy finally reached over and entangled his fingers in mine. Tightening our snuggle on the couch, I felt so warm and so cozy. I couldn't even tell you who won the game that day. I was in another world, wrapped up in those big strong arms.

We both had assumed that we would be together again for the Seahawks game that next afternoon. Deciding to meet at a bar, I met him there, as he was now able to drive himself around. Progress. Both dressed in our Seahawks jerseys, both diehard fans, we were eager to watch Seattle win. As we watched the game over cocktails, we shared kisses between plays. I struggled to keep my hands off him, loving the sexual chemistry that was building between us. This was our third time out together, and the more time I spent with him, the more I was ready to throw this guy down on the bed and screw his brains out.

The game was a blowout by fourth quarter, and not in the Seahawks favor (not a huge surprise there). Too horny to watch the rest of the game, we made a break for the doors, wanting to get back to his place, excited to be naked and in each other's arms. Rushing in the door, we left a trail of clothes to his bedroom, both of us so eager. Climbing into his bed, I lay down, with him right behind me. As he gathered me in his arms, I felt his cock slide inside me. He felt so good.

Just as I was beginning to get lost in the moment, he quickly jumped off me and hurried to the bathroom. An instant later I heard him throwing up. Ewww, I thought, this guy can't hold his alcohol. Not a good sign. After a break in the sounds from the bathroom, I hollered to him, asking if he was okay. "Yes," he muttered.

Shaking my head, I then heard the shower turn on. Tiptoeing to the bathroom, I stuck my head in the doorway and saw he was leaning over the shower and still getting sick. First time I had ever seen someone get sick in the shower versus the toilet. Interesting choice. I closed the door before he noticed me and began to get dressed. My plan was to head home and leave this day behind me. Disappointed for sure, I had hoped for a different outcome from this date.

Just as I slipped my last shoe on, he emerged from the bathroom looking haggard at best. "Where do you think you are going?" he demanded. Not thinking this moment needed an explanation, I ventured into it anyway, pointing out that he was puking and the sexual mood had disappeared quite quickly. I was going to go home and try to forget the evening.

Pleading with me, he begged, "Please don't leave. I'll be damned if I let you walk away not getting laid properly." Laughing at the look on his face, I was amused that he was so hell-bent on making sure I knew he was a good fuck. Reluctantly I agreed to stay and climbed back into bed. As I was telling him we could maybe try again in the morning, I heard him start to snore. Rolling my eyes, I sarcastically thought, How romantic.

Early in the morning hours, I woke up to feel Fun Time Guy's hands on my body. Wide awake and instantly turned on, I responded hungrily. I wanted him. With one hand pinching my nipple and the other grabbing my ass cheeks, he raised his lips to meet mine and passionately kissed me. Running my hands through his hair, I felt my hips already moving and grinding against his naked body. As he rolled on top of me, I felt his hands all over me, and I knew this time was different. His stiff cock slowly slid into me and began pumping back and forth, sliding easily in my wet pussy. His cock was so hard and it fit so well, almost as if it was made for me.

Our bodies moved as one together, harder and deeper with each thrust. As he was inside me, I felt his warm lips kissing my neck and ear, making me hold him tighter and pull him in deeper. Feeling the urge to straddle him, I gently pushed him off me and told him to lie on his back. Climbing on top of him, I sat down, lowering myself onto his rock-hard cock. Rocking back and forth, my clit rubbing against him, I was lost in the feeling. Pulling my legs up into the sitting position, Fun Time Guy immediately grabbed them, helping me rock faster. Building to the climax, I felt myself cumming. As my moans got louder, I heard him start to groan with pleasure. Together we came. Collapsing onto the bed, panting and smiling, I mentioned that he had been worth the wait. He laughed. As he pulled me close, I slid into the crook of his arm and lay my head on his chest. He felt so good, and I could have stayed in that moment forever. "We fit," he whispered.

Chapter 25

I feel like we spent the remainder of his two weeks off in bed together. When I think back at our early memories as a couple, I adored the times when we were able to sleep late on the weekends, a tangled mess of arms and legs under the covers. I discovered a lot about Fun Time Guy during that time. Not only was he extremely talented in the bedroom, but outside the bedroom he was actually fun to hang out with too.

Telling me goodbye, as he headed out for his two weeks of work in Alaska, I surprised myself by feeling sad to see him go. It had been a long time since I had experienced that true sentimental feeling. A little scared by my intense feelings, I brushed them off and went to spend the day with my daughter. I needed to regroup and get Fun Time Guy off my mind.

Monday at work was the usual grind. Appointments and meetings kept me busy and preoccupied; nevertheless, I was surprised at how often I had thoughts of him creep into my head. Every time I thought of the past two weeks, I found myself smiling. Walking back into my office, I noticed a beautiful bouquet of flowers on my desk. Intrigued, I noticed the flowers were nestled in a small white vase that was shaped like two snowmen hugging each other. Pulling the card out of the bouquet, smiling, I read the message. “Had a wonderful two weeks, can’t wait to see you when I get home,” and it was signed *The Puker*. Laughing out loud, I held the card to my heart, very happy and warm inside. Completely caught off guard, one of my managers popped her head in my office at that moment. “Flowers?” she questioned, a sly smile on her face. Knowing that she was looking for answers, but I wasn’t prepared to give any, I simply answered, “Yep.” Sensing she would get nothing from me, she rolled her eyes and went back to work. I texted Fun Time Guy. “Thank you for the flowers, they are beautiful.” A heart emoji came back.

As I felt my feelings start to deepen for Fun Time Guy, I was hypersensitive to the fact that choosing a serious, committed relationship with someone you met on an online adult website had some serious drawbacks. Thinking ahead, there would come a day where I would want to introduce Fun Time Guy to my daughter, to my family, and to my friends. To show them that I was finally moving on and had found someone that I had serious feelings for. But how would I even introduce him? Would I have to lie about how we met? The only answer I could come up with was yes. Just as I had been fearful of telling even my closest friends, there was no way I could tell my parents or my daughter the truth. If they knew, no one would ever take us seriously, and they would look at our relationship like a joke. Some might even question the security of my daughter and judge me as a poor mother. I couldn't bear the thought of that happening.

I knew that if we continued to pursue this growing relationship, we would have to pledge to never reveal the true way we met. Yes, we could still say we met online, but just not reveal the site. It was too risky.

Dating someone with a schedule like Fun Time Guy's also comes with its share of challenges. Not only did he work in Alaska, but he worked two weeks on and two weeks off, so when he came back into town, he had no obligations for two weeks. While two weeks off at a time was great for him, it was exhausting for me. I still had my daily obligations, I still had to work, and I was still a mom to a busy kiddo. Desperately I tried to keep a "normal" schedule when he was in town, but it was always a challenge. When he would finally head back to work, I found myself almost relieved, yearning for a good night's sleep, an alcohol detox, and healthy food. During those times he was in town, I called it the two-week binge.

A two-week lull without sex was the biggest drawback to him leaving. With our sex life thriving, you'd think him leaving would allow me to rest my body so it was ready when he returned, but that wasn't the case. I wanted him daily, to feel him inside me every morning and every night. Clearly, I was a woman coming into my sexual peak, and he satisfied my every need. Except when he wasn't there to satisfy my every need. We quickly made adjustments to our schedule. Several times a week we had sexy time over the phone. Crawling into bed naked, with just my phone, it didn't take long before we would work ourselves up into a sexual frenzy, almost as good if we had been in the same bed together. Talking dirty, touching ourselves, we could cum together, then fall asleep.

Chapter 26

When you decide to take risks, you open up a whole new set of questions.

Another question that had to be asked as our relationship was taking form was: where do you draw the line for sexual expectations with each other? We knew from our meeting circumstances that we were both highly sexual people and that we both had experienced erotic and wild adventures with different partners. Was this something that we would continue to try to add into our relationship? With all these complicated questions, I was thankful of the ability to communicate freely with Fun Time Guy. Talking openly about any topic was always encouraged and easy to do. Part of me felt as if we developed this characteristic from the website. Funny as it sounds, but when you are discussing taboo subjects with complete strangers, it makes a normal conversation seem somewhat easy.

We both approached the sexual subject in a similar fashion. Recognizing that we were very sexual people, and that we enjoyed creative and spontaneous moments, we could talk through the possibility of periodically doing something outside the box. With that, he hinted that a threesome, or perhaps being with another couple, might be erotic and fun to try. Rolling my eyes and laughing, I noted this was a typical guy response. He then followed up his statement, reassuring me that if I was never interested or comfortable in doing anything outside the "norm" again, that our sex life was amazing and fulfilling.

On one impulsive evening, Fun Time Guy and I decided to log in to the website, and this time be the couple looking for another couple. If nothing else, we could have a stimulating evening of erotic chatting with some strangers, turning us both on, ending up in the bedroom sexually satisfied. Logging in for the first time in almost six months, what a different feeling it was logging in next to my boyfriend. Even though we both had been extremely honest about our time on the site, I had always been alone when surfing through the site, and here I was with a guy by my side. As I went to the profile area, I changed the drop-down box from single woman looking for single men to a couple looking for a couple. Next step, we had to go through and update our profile description, which he looked at me to do. Laughing, I immediately wrote, "Average normal couple seeks the same for a good time. No friends needed, only benefits." Clicking submit, I remembered when I had done this earlier in the year. Wow, how things had changed. Regarding the profile photo, we decided based on my previous experiences to skip it. Never can be too cautious.

We didn't have to wait long at all before we received a plethora of messages as well as online chats. It was fun to have someone next to me, two minds to help with responses. The hours flew by as we chatted with other couples. Some seeming as normal as us, and possibly if this had been a different situation, they probably could have probably been our friends. I also call ourselves "normal" in relative terms. While we both knew that not everyone would understand what we were doing, on the website we felt like the more vanilla ones. While there were "normal" couples, there were also the usual over-the-top kinky people that I was glad to say were too kinky for us both. Those chats were deleted, and once again we narrowed the responses down to a more manageable number.

One couple kept our interest piqued, and we decided to share our number to begin chatting over the phone. Between Fun Time Guy and myself, we had decided that if we had found a situation like this, that I would share my number and call the shots. I was more comfortable with this decision based on several things: I trusted myself. Not to say that I didn't trust Fun Time Guy, but things were still new, and I wasn't going to take any chances. The second reason was pure vanity. I wanted to find a couple where I was prettier than the other girl. My insecurity was showing, but it was important to be honest with myself and with him. I didn't want all of us to be in the same room with a drop-dead gorgeous girl and both of the guys wanting to do her, and here I would be in the corner, naked, yelling, *What about me?* Fun Time Guy thought this was the funniest thing ever, but again, he wanted to ensure that I felt entirely comfortable from start to finish, so he kissed me on top of my head and said, "Whatever you want."

I found out through the texts that I was chatting with the guy of the couple. He was very nice and respectful, understanding that this could be a touchy situation for some. Different from looking for a single guy, you had more rules to cover, ensuring that everyone was on the same page. My thoughts drifted back to the boyfriend who ended up lying to his girlfriend. I did not want to add more drama to my life; we were just looking for a good time. He and I agreed to meet up the following weekend. For the main rules, we also agreed on a full swap in the same room. Having no idea what that entailed when I started this process, I now knew what that meant. We were both open to having sex with the other partner (me with him) and Fun Time Guy with his wife. Same room was just what it sounded like—we had to all be together in one room, not in separate rooms, where you had no idea what was going on. To me, that would drive me crazy not knowing.

That Friday evening, driving to a local hotel where we would meet the other couple, Fun Time Guy and I went through what the evening might look like, asking each other if anything was off-limits. Fun Time Guy had done this before, and he was more confident going into this situation. I was nervous and excited, very similar to how I had felt in the past with each one of my adventures. But I knew this one was going to be so much different. I was with a guy that I was falling in love with, and I had no idea if anything was off-limits until I experienced it. I tried to convey that to Fun Time Guy and make it make sense, or the sense that it was in my head. He squeezed my hand in the car. "We can stop any time you aren't comfortable." I smiled, nodded, and squeezed his hand back.

We met them in the hotel bar; we all needed a little liquid courage for the deed that we were about to embark on. They beat us to the bar, and waved us over to their table when we walked in. Again, quite the normal-looking couple, he was about five ten and handsome in a rugged way. He had a goatee and was dressed in a flannel shirt and blue jeans. She was pretty, with an olive complexion and long, dark, wavy hair. She was dressed very sexy in a low-cut shirt and tight blue jeans. They were both about our age. As we sipped our drinks, they let us know that they had gotten the key to the hotel room, so we were all set. Whenever we were ready.

Ready. A relative word in this situation. I wasn't sure if I was going to be completely turned on or going to puke. Either was possible. Walking into the room, I took note of my surroundings. A large king bed was glaring at me from the middle of the room and a pull-out sleeper sofa was on my right. Your typical hotel room. Feeling slightly awkward as we entered the room, I decided to make the first move and get this party started. I kept thinking I might feel better once the game was on. I walked up to the female and began kissing her, slowly and passionately, while running my hands along her body. Lifting her shirt up over her arms, I sat her down on the sofa and continued to kiss her while running my hands across her tits. Immediately aware of a set of arms reaching around me, I looked up to see her husband behind me. Pulling me toward him, he guided me over to the bed. He began kissing me, slowly flicking his tongue in and out of my mouth. As he started undressing me, I did the same to him. Shirt for shirt, pants for pants. I slid my panties off and lay down on the bed. As I lay down, I glanced over to Fun Time Guy and her. He was sitting on the couch, where she had straddled him, and they were passionately kissing. Quickly I took my pulse on it all, and overall I still felt good with the situation at hand.

Husband was quickly on top of me as I lay on the bed. Moaning, he made his way down and began to softly lick me. While it felt good, I couldn't help but again look over at Fun Time Guy. It was like my mind was in two different places. I wanted to enjoy myself, but I also wanted to monitor the situation unfolding on the couch. I wanted Fun Time Guy to enjoy himself, but in the end I needed to know that after this interaction we would feel the same way about each other. The wife had slid down off his lap and onto her knees. She had his cock in her mouth, and I noticed his eyes were closed. Sensing my gaze, he opened them for just a moment, smiled at me, and then closed his eyes once again.

Back into the moment, I pulled Husband up from where he was camped out and told him to fuck me. He nodded, kissing me again. He tasted like me, and this time I closed my eyes, waiting for him to be inside me. I felt his cock plunge into me, and I was pleasantly shocked by the size of him. He had some girth to him. I raised my legs, and he went to work. He was a good lay, and I found myself really getting into it. As he flipped me over onto all fours, I found myself facing Fun Time Guy and her. She was straddling him again, this time with his cock inside her. She was bouncing up and down on his cock, while her tits were in his mouth. She was loud, making a lot of noise, which I found a bit irritating. But smiling to myself, I just thought about the funny things that bother me and the things that don't.

Feeling the husband getting ready to cum, I rocked my hips, matching his thrusts. Moans escaping from his mouth, he fell to the bed, exhausted from the explosion. They were also finishing up on the couch, as I recognized Fun Time Guy's subtle moans telling me he was ready to cum. As I watched him cum, I couldn't help but be extremely turned on at how sexy and handsome he was. He lay down on the couch, stretching out, enjoying the moment. Sensing the moment, I watched Wife inch her body over to Fun Time Guy and cuddle herself up in the crook of his arm and drape her arm over his chest. I didn't like that at all.

In an instant I couldn't breathe. I was on my feet, immediately blurting out that it was time to leave. I felt all eyes on me, wondering why the abruptness, but I didn't care. She was in my spot, with my guy. I hadn't minded the blow job, the kissing, or the sex, but I did mind the cuddling. I was immediately jealous and wanted out of the moment. I made eye contact with Fun Time Guy, and I could see in his eyes that he was concerned. He jumped up, got dressed, and we said a quick goodbye and found ourselves in the hallway before I could exhale. I was so glad in the moment that we left the room that he didn't speak. He just wrapped his arms around me and held me. For the first time in about a year, I completely acted like a girl. I burst into tears, for reasons that I couldn't even articulate. I was feeling things that I never felt before, and it was incredibly overwhelming.

We really didn't speak until we were in the car driving home. He timidly asked if I was okay. I laughed at his concerned expression and nodded. "Everything was good until the moment she tried to cuddle with you. She was in my spot. I hadn't realized how much I cared about you until it went past sex, to more of an intimate touch. Does that even make sense?" I asked him. He nodded and tried to explain that it hadn't been intimate to him; it was just sex and then they both had lay down. Even though I knew that was the case, I also knew it was near impossible for him to understand the feeling that I felt. Men and women are just different, especially in a sexual situation. Fun Time Guy reached for my hand and held it tightly the entire way home.

Chapter 27

There were too many pivotal moments to count over the next few months with Fun Time Guy. Over lunch one day, he told me about an ex-girlfriend who had called him, wanting to go out. He told her that he had met someone special, so he wouldn't be able to see her anymore.

"Does this mean we are exclusive?" I asked.

We sealed it with a kiss. We had also taken our first trip together in those early months, on a road trip to Whistler, British Columbia. Spending hours skiing during the day and curled up at night in front of the fireplace, we learned that we traveled well together, which I believe is key to any great relationship. If you can spend time together in a hotel room, airport, and rental car, and still get along, you get a great idea of how that individual will react to stress and spontaneity in real life. Do they like to do the same things, eat at the same type of restaurants, and relax in the same way?

Logging on to the website now seemed to be old news. It had been months since I had seen my inbox, and I found that the more time I spent with Fun Time Guy, the less time I needed to chase that online erotic feeling. My heart was beginning to tell me that it felt healed and that I was ready to develop feelings and perhaps even fall in love again. After my divorce, I had told myself I would never marry again, but I did know that I was still interested in finding my life partner. I loved the feeling of always having someone in your life to share things with and to have a best friend by your side. Perhaps Fun Time Guy might be that guy? I began to wonder.

I think I had mentioned earlier that Fun Time Guy was not exactly my type. Physically, I could easily say that he was my ideal match, but there were other characteristics he possessed, ones that I had to decide if I could tolerate for the long run.

Starting with our backgrounds, he and I grew up very differently. I grew up in a middle-class, modest home with my family: mother, stepfather (my father died when I was nine), an older brother, and older sister. We were all very close, even to this day we are a tight-knit family. Living in the same small town for my entire school career, I had the same friends, played in the same neighborhoods, and got into moderate trouble growing up. The craziest thing I remember doing was throwing a house party while my parents were out of town. After graduating from high school, I went away to college a couple hours from home and then started my life in the hospitality world. Pretty vanilla, I would say.

Now, Fun Time Guy grew up very different. He grew up in several places: Tacoma, Washington; Houston, Texas; and

Fairbanks, Alaska. Living with his mom, stepdad, and younger brother for most of his life, he summered in Alaska with his biological father and his half sister. To be honest, his family tree was more like a forest, branching out in all different directions, with half siblings here and there, as well as friends that called themselves "sibling." It took some serious studying to understand who was who. After high school he struggled with the path he would take, either becoming a delinquent or joining the army. Thankfully he chose the army, where he was successful as a Ranger and made some great lifelong "brothers" who assisted in setting him on the right path.

His sexual past was also quite lengthy. Telling me that he had received the advice from his father to "bang them all" as he was growing up. Once again that double standard came into play. While I had dated the same high school boyfriend for three years, he was hitting everything that had tits. When I asked him why he never had any kids or married anyone, he basically told me that he had been afraid that he would lose the kids in a divorce as well as all the money he had worked so hard for. Realizing at that moment that he had never been around truly healthy relationships, I wondered if he could ever be in one himself. All very important things that I needed to consider when choosing someone I wanted to spend my life with. Isn't it ironic that now I was silently judging someone on their sexual past as one of the predictors for a successful long-term partner? Men do this all the time, which is why women often aren't honest about their sexual past.

Besides the major background differences, he was also loud (partially deaf from his days in the army) and spoke with his hands. While it doesn't seem like a deal-breaker, one had to fully accept this characteristic, or it might be something that would drive me crazy ten years down the road. We went to dinner one night, and when he excused himself to use the restroom, the couple at the table seated next to us leaned over to me and asked if I was okay. Confused, I nodded and asked why. They had heard his loud voice, saw his hands waving the air, and assumed he was yelling at me. I still chuckle at that one. Everyone has something they may not love about their partner. But the ultimate answer to the conundrum of whether you can make it is: do I want to live without them?

I made a list of all of the differences we had, and shook my head when I thought about how crazy he made me. I knew up-front that some of those traits were bound to irritate me, but any successful relationship included two imperfect people.

No one is perfect, but you must ask yourself if the good qualities outweigh the bad ones. I think that is the most important question. Some people are their own worst enemy, picking apart every single dating option until there's no one left because their standard is perfection. Those people aren't looking for a mate, they're looking for a robot!

Fun Time Guy loves fiercely. He is one of the most loyal people I have ever met. He is incredibly affectionate, always giving me a kiss, holding my hand, or just making me feel beautiful. I also know that he would jump in front of a bus to save me or my daughter. He is a protector and makes me feel safe, which as a woman I believe is one of the most important traits he could possess. His sense of humor keeps me laughing, and his sarcasm can almost match mine. Almost. Fun Time Guy is amazing in bed, having just the right amount of kink to drive me wild. I felt as though I had met my match with Fun Time Guy.

Six months into the relationship, it was finally time to introduce Fun Time Guy to my daughter. She was five at this time, and I felt as though she would be okay meeting Mommy's friend. Fun Time Guy had been nothing but respectful, honoring and understanding of my timeline. He never pressured me, nor did he question my rules. Those rules would also continue to exist, even once he had met her. I was adamant that he was not allowed to stay the night while she was home, nor could we kiss in front of her, etc. Not yet. This had to be something that we eased her into.

We met for dinner at Spaghetti Factory, as I told myself that a public place was a much easier place for an introduction. I, of course, drove myself and my daughter, and Fun Time Guy was going to meet us there. I explained to her on the ride to the restaurant that she was going to meet Mommy's friend. Basically not caring and somewhat clueless, she nodded and happily continued playing with her toys from her car seat. I smiled, trying to ease my nervousness, even though in all my time online dating I had never been as nervous as I was this moment. I think as a parent, especially a divorced parent, you are always wondering what damage this moment could cause your child. Will they wonder who this new man is? What if they don't like him? What if he's awful with children?

Will meeting Mommy's friend cause her more emotional issues when she grows up as a teen? Will she need counseling because of me? We've all heard the stories of blended families and the trauma kids experienced. As a single mom I was very focused on making sure every situation involving my daughter was closely monitored and planned. So, on that day my stomach was in knots!

Walking into the restaurant, I spotted Fun Time Guy right away. I was holding my daughter's hand, and he was smiling at both of us. It was an odd feeling not to greet him with my normal affectionate kiss, but I knew he understood. And that was the first test. He honored my silent approach and was intuitive enough to know I would not want to show affection or take anything away from my daughter's perception or interaction with him. I would not want her to feel confusion or even jealousy, like so many kids do.

He immediately bent down and held out his hand to my daughter. "Nice to meet you," he said, smiling. Holding my breath, I watched her smile back at him and politely shake his hand. Then in an instant, completely oblivious to the magnitude of this situation, she pointed to the kid area in the restaurant and asked to go play. Fun Time Guy looked at me and mouthed if he could take her. I nodded.

He offered his hand, she immediately took it, and then walked off toward the play area. I could see Fun Time Guy talking with her, and she was nodding and then laughed at something he must have said. Feeling a lump in my throat and my eyes fill with happy tears, I let out the breath I hadn't realized I had been holding, and sank into my seat. I watched them play in the kids' area and saw how natural their first meeting was. My heart was happy.

Over dinner that weekend, with just Fun Time Guy and myself, he told me he loved me. With tears in his eyes, he held my hands and told me how important I had become to him in such a short amount of time. My heart had told me that this moment had been coming soon, especially with him meeting my daughter. That had been a huge step for our relationship.

In this moment, we both confessed our growing feelings to each other. It was easy to look at his face, into his eyes, and tell him I loved him as well. I felt closer to him than I had ever felt with any other person in my whole life. We did fit. We both had shortcomings that were made whole because of each other. When he held me, I felt a feeling of home and comfort. Feeling celebratory, we ordered a bottle of champagne. Clinking our glasses, we toasted to the future.

Chapter 28

Fun Time Guy and I decided to move in together; it would mark our two-year anniversary. Our love was strong, and I could feel how much he cared for my daughter like she was his own. They had a special relationship, and I loved watching it grow. Having no kids of his own, he struggled to get it right at times, but he was able to share his life experiences with her, guiding her to understand right and wrong.

He moved into my townhouse, where we lived for a year before purchasing our first home together as a family. The house wasn't too far from my ex-husband's house, so we were able to co-parent quite easily, putting less strain on my daughter. We added two pups to the household chaos, feeling as though we were complete, and it was an exhilarating time!

Our families were extremely happy for us and for our relationship. My family adored Fun Time Guy and knew he was a good fit for me. They had been worried about me after my divorce, so seeing me happy and cared for brought them peace. Of course I still wondered if they would feel differently if they knew how we had met. As we had promised to each other, we never had shared where we met, telling people only that we met online, but never sharing more than that. I don't think anyone would have assumed it was on an adult website. It remained our little secret.

His family welcomed me with open arms. I think they had secretly always worried about whether Fun Time Guy would ever settle down. Also, his chances of finding someone successful and "normal" seemed far off as well, so I like to think that they were pleasantly surprised with his choice. They might even like me better than him. While we had no plans to get married, they knew that I was going to take care of their son forever.

Fun Time Guy and I traveled the world together. We both loved to explore new places, eat new food, and meet new people. On international trips, we normally traveled alone, just the two of us, but simple in-country trips we did as a family with my daughter. Italy, Vietnam, Thailand, too many countries to name, only brought us closer. Traveling together was extremely easy for us, both wanting an equal balance of lounge time and explore and adventure time, like having a new best friend who just fit like a glove. Now, years later, the best advice I can give to anyone looking for their life partner is to take a chance. Be open to the possibility that happiness with someone could lie outside of your preconceived notions, your list of qualities you desire in a mate, and your comfort zone.

We've had a beautiful relationship! But please don't let me fool you into thinking our relationship has been all sunshine and rainbows. Like any relationship, we had and continue to have many struggles, some of them major. For one, although he is probably not as much of a hothead as he was when he was younger, he is still very much an asshole during arguments, and he struggles to fight fair. I have huge expectations, sometimes too big, and I expected him to live up to them immediately. At first, I didn't allow time for us to adjust, learn, and grow together, but I continue to adapt. We've had to sacrifice and learn so many new things, compromising at times when neither wanted to. But I believe that the secret is that we both want to get better. We both want to continue to grow together. Not just one of us, but both.

When I think back to our initial meeting on the website, I still believe that if we had been able to meet in person shortly after starting to chat, we probably would not still be together. I do think we would have met up, had amazing sex, but then we would have gone our separate ways, just as we had done with so many before each other. Timing is everything! And I still feel the big difference in our relationship was that we created a friendship first. We were able to develop feelings that ran deeper than just the sexual experience. When we began to talk, we learned more about the other person and began to respect each other and grow as friends.

But let's not downplay the physical attraction!

Acknowledging that we did, in fact, meet on a sex website, we are confident in saying that sex was and continues to be something that is very important in our relationship. Now, instead of exploring new scenarios with different partners, we get to create and explore any new scenarios with each other. We are best friends, and we are great lovers.

Chapter 29

It seems when life is going well and you find yourself in a comfortable groove is when your world gets rocked. As if there is someone waiting to throw you a curveball just to make sure you are paying attention. I feel it is a way to prevent us from taking things or people for granted.

Fun Time Guy was away at work in Alaska, and it was a normal, hectic workday for me. I was busy prepping for a presentation for some colleagues when I had to use the restroom. Finishing up, I wiped, looking down, realizing there was a large amount of blood on the tissue paper. Enough blood to startle me. Concerned, and thinking that I needed to maybe call my doctor, I stood up to wash my hands. As I stood in front of the sink and looked in the mirror, I leaned in closer, noticing very small red dots on my face underneath my eyes. Those hadn't been there this morning, I thought. With my concern increasing, I went to my office to call my doctor. Hearing his voice mail, I decided better safe than sorry and I would call the emergency room at the nearby hospital. The receptionist answered right away, and I proceeded to tell her about the strange symptoms I had just discovered. Hearing a bit of concern in her voice, she told me that I should get to the emergency room right away.

Hanging up the phone, taking a calming breath, I thought this is crazy, I feel fine, maybe just a little tired, but that was nothing new. I quickly handed off my presentation to my next manager in line, who looked less than thrilled to now be giving a speech, but I had too much on my mind to care. Throwing on my jacket, I headed out of work, and decided it was a beautiful day to just walk to the hospital. It was only twelve city blocks, and besides that, I didn't really want to have to move my car to another garage and pay another fee. Parking in the city was expensive. The walk was a breath of fresh air.

I let the girl at the front desk know I had just called, and it was recommended I come in. I reiterated my symptoms, filled out the required paperwork, and waited. Quickly, they called me back and started asking more questions about my symptoms. Taking note of the little pink dots on my face, they checked my hands and feet, which unknown to me, were covered in the same spots.

"What are they?" I asked.

"Petechiae," the nurse said. "Broken blood vessels."

They checked me in, got me a gown and a bed, and proceeded to run tests. They were unsure of what was wrong with me, but as I listened to their banter between them, I heard words like cancer, leukemia, and AIDS. AIDS? Immediately the past year of my life ran through my head. Yes, I had been safe, and used protection, but I had been with multiple partners. Protection wasn't always guaranteed. Had I been careless? Had I been selfish? Was I being punished for following my sexual adventure? Beginning to panic, I started making a few phone calls to let others know where I was. My first call was to my ex-husband. I told him everything I knew thus far, which wasn't much, but I wanted to ensure that he was able to pick up our daughter from school that day.

"Of course," he responded. "Please keep me posted."

I then called Fun Time Guy, who was in the middle of his shift at work. After telling him where I was and about my symptoms, I had to hold back the tears when I heard the intense concern in his voice. Suddenly he seemed so far away. I had yet to cry, and I didn't want to start now. It would just make him worry more. I reassured him that I felt fine, that it was probably nothing, and that I would call him back as soon as I had any update. Immediately he told me that he was going to try to find a flight out of Alaska to be with me, but I told him no, not until we knew something definite.

My mom was next on the list to call, and in true fashion, I burst into tears as soon as I heard her voice. Something about a mother's love and their voice can make you feel like you're ten years old again. Hearing that I was in the hospital was enough for her. She hung up the phone and was on her way. She arrived as they were still conducting tests. When she and my brother walked in together, I had never felt more relieved.

Still unsure of why I was bleeding internally, the doctors discovered that my blood was not clotting and that my platelet count was dangerously low. A normal woman my age has approximately 250,000 to 500,000 platelets in their body at all times, but my count was ten. Not ten thousand, but ten. They ordered an immediate blood transfusion to help my blood clot and stop the bleeding. One of my doctors had told me that he was shocked I had not been bleeding out of my nose, ears, or eyes. My body, for whatever reason, was attacking my platelets, making it impossible for me to stop bleeding. If I had shaved my legs that day and accidentally cut myself, I could have died.

My mom called Fun Time Guy for me. She updated him on my situation, still not knowing what was causing my condition. He was panicked and told her that he needed to be with me. She calmed him down and assured him that she and my brother were there and would keep him updated. The nurse, overhearing our conversation, mentioned to me that due to the severity of my symptoms, only immediate family and spouses would be allowed in the room, unfortunately not boyfriends.

Tests continued. Ultrasounds, MRIs, and more blood transfusions. I was going on day three in the hospital with still no diagnosis. My ex-husband brought my daughter by, and I was determined not to cry when I saw her because I didn't want her to worry any more than she had to. The good thing was, I really didn't even look sick, so it was much easier to convince her that everything was all right.

So many flowers were delivered to my room, it smelled like a flower shop. I felt so loved, even when I was so scared. The realization that nothing else matters but your health hits you hard when you are facing a situation such as this. Truly it is not the car you drive, or how much money you make, but the people you love and love you are what matters. You really cannot take anything else with you.

After a week in the hospital, the doctors were able to get my bleeding under control. With the use of steroids and more infusions, my platelet count was slowly responding, increasing to over twenty thousand. They finally had given me a diagnosis, ITP—idiopathic thrombocytopenic purpura. It is a rare autoimmune disease that may be chronic in adults, but doctors really have no idea what causes it. Relieved that it wasn't cancer or AIDS, I said another silent prayer, this time in thanks. I was blessed to be recovering.

Coming home, I was overjoyed to be back in my surroundings. My ex-husband had brought my daughter over to welcome me home, and although she couldn't stay with me quite yet, I was overjoyed just to be able to hold her. My mom was also planning on staying with me until Fun Time Guy got home the following day. I was grateful for her company and her love. She was always there for me when I needed her.

I couldn't wait to see Fun Time Guy. He had landed and was headed home. My mom had left an hour earlier, needing to get back to her own house, and I had assured her that I would be fine in the hour or two before he got home. When he walked in, he dropped his bag and scooped me up in his arms. No words were spoken, we just held each other, knowing how lucky we were to be able to do this. Pulling back from me, he looked into my eyes, wiping my tears away, and tucking my hair behind my ear.

"I love you so much, baby," he cried, with tears streaming down his face. He started to apologize for not being there for me, but I quickly stopped him.

"I had my mom there, and I knew I was going to be okay. It would have taken you days to try to get home from work." I then explained that the hospital would not have even let him in, as only immediate family and spouses were allowed. Shaking his head, I could tell he felt guilty.

"You should be my wife," he whispered.

"I am good, and getting healthier every day. We are good, and I love you so much," I said. Embracing again, I could feel his heartbeat against mine.

As the months passed and I healed, everything went back to normal, even though inside it felt as if so much had changed. Sometimes it takes a crisis, health issue, or a loss in the family to make you aware of how precious and fleeting life really is. We only have this moment.

We began traveling again and booked a trip to Arizona to the healing desert. Scottsdale, Arizona, had been one of our favorite spots to travel to together, as it was a quick plane ride to beautiful weather, good friends, and plenty of outdoor activities. It was also always a great escape from the dreary, cold weather of Seattle. One of our first trips together had been a golf trip to Scottsdale, so it held special meaning and fond memories for us. This particular time, we were traveling there to watch the Seattle Seahawks play the Arizona Cardinals. At least once a year, we tried to travel to an away game on the Seahawks schedule, either to experience a game in a new city, or to a place where we could pair the game with golf and a visit with friends.

This trip, we planned to start the weekend with a hike in Sedona. Fun Time Guy and I had never been to the area, so it was something new to see, which we always appreciated. Joining us on the hike was a close girlfriend of mine and her cousin, so not only were we able to enjoy some outdoor exercise, but also a great visit along the way.

The legendary views of the red rocks in Sedona were stunning, with picturesque settings around every corner. As we reached the summit, nestled in between the formations and built into the rocks stood a majestic cathedral. If you've seen it before, you understand its beauty, but if not, it is worth the hike. The views once you reach the Chapel of the Holy Cross were even more spectacular than on the way up, so we paused to take it all in. As I gazed out at the landscape in front of me, I had no idea that at that very moment my girlfriend was aiming her camera directly at me, preparing to capture a day that would be one of the best days of my life. As I looked out over the formations, blessed to be there, I turned around to see Fun Time Guy on one knee, holding a small box out in front of him.

"Marry me. Be my wife," he said.

Feeling my eyes well up with tears, I had no words. I just nodded and pulled him to me. It was all so surreal! Taking the ring from the box, he held my hand and slid the beautiful ring on my finger.

I had known this was the man that I was going to spend forever with, but now it was going to be made official. Throughout our relationship, we both had always said that we didn't need marriage to confirm that our love was forever; however, now we both felt in our hearts that it was important to be husband and wife. To pledge to our family and friends and to God that we were here for each other till death do us part.

The moments that most women want to forget and slide under the rug preceded the proposal. How often do we see young girls, or even middle-aged women, who seek the proposal yet want to cover up and forget the sexual adventures, or what they categorize as "mistakes," to reach the final destination? If there's any message that I have for those women it is that it's the journey itself and the kaleidoscope of experiences that make up who we are. It's not just the successes but the so-called failures, the mistakes, the lapses in judgment, the free will, and yes, even the moments of pure abandon with no strings attached that make us who we are! Marriage should not feel like the final destination, even if it's what you want. The path of life is just as important. Give yourself permission to live and to enjoy your life without judgment!

My adventures, my need to quench a sexual desire, and all of my explorations, had all been so amazing, satisfying, and erotic, yet had led me here. They led me to my life partner, but they also led me to confidence, self-fulfillment, and to love. They led me to him. I wouldn't change a thing.

About the Author

Jana Smith is an author, speaker, and hospitality executive who writes about taking risks and living her best life. As a single mother and a thirtysomething-year-old woman, Jana embarked on a self-discovering journey and shares her adventures in her first book.

A wiseass and romantic at heart, she convinces her readers to chase their dreams as well as their happy endings, with no apologies.

Raised in a small town outside of Seattle, Jana now lives and works in the beautiful Rocky Mountain state of Colorado. Sharing her life with her husband and her seventeen-year-old daughter, she fights daily to be a strong woman role model and instill in her daughter that she can do anything she puts her mind to.